Second Workshop on Computational Research in Linguistic Typology (SIGTYP 2020)

Online
19 November 2020

ISBN: 978-1-7138-2003-1

Printed from e-media with permission by:

Curran Associates, Inc.
57 Morehouse Lane
Red Hook, NY 12571

Some format issues inherent in the e-media version may also appear in this print version.

Association for Computational Linguistics
209 N. Eighth Street
Stroudsburg, Pennsylvania 18360

Phone: 1-570-476-8006
Fax: 1-570-476-0860

acl@aclweb.org

Additional copies of this publication are available from:

Curran Associates, Inc.
57 Morehouse Lane
Red Hook, NY 12571 USA
Phone: 845-758-0400
Fax: 845-758-2633
Email: curran@proceedings.com
Web: www.proceedings.com

SIGTYP 2020

Second Workshop on Computational Research in Linguistic Typology

Proceedings of the Workshop

November 19, 2020
Online

Introduction

SIGTYP 2020 is the second edition of the workshop for typology-related research and its integration into multilingual Natural Language Processing (NLP), which was inaugurated last year at ACL 2019. The workshop is co-located with the 2020 Conference on Empirical Methods in Natural Language Processing, which takes place virtually this year. Our workshop includes a shared task on typological feature prediction, which saw the participation of 5 teams for a total of 8 systems submitted.

The final program of SIGTYP contains 5 keynote talks, 6 shared task papers, 11 extended abstracts, selected among a large number of non-archival submissions, and 3 papers from "Findings of ACL: EMNLP 2020". This workshop would not have been possible without the hard work of its program committee, to whom we would like to express our gratitude. We should also thank our invited speakers, Miriam Butt, Yulia Tsvetkov, Richard Sproat, Bill Croft, Harald Hammarström, for their irreplaceable contribution to our program. The workshop is generously sponsored by Google and by the European Research Council (ERC) Consolidator Grant LEXICAL (no. 648909).

Please find more details on the SIGTYP 2020 website: `https://sigtyp.github.io/ws2020.html`

Organizing Committee:

Arya D. McCarthy, Johns Hopkins University
Edoardo M. Ponti, Mila Montreal and University of Cambridge
Ekaterina Vylomova, University of Melbourne
Haim Dubossarsky, University of Cambridge
Ivan Vulić, University of Cambridge

Steering Committee:

Anna Korhonen, University of Cambridge
Eitan Grossman, Hebrew University of Jerusalem
Roi Reichart, Technion - Israel Institute of Technology
Ryan Cotterell, ETH Zurich and University of Cambridge
Yevgeni Berzak, MIT

Program Committee:

Johannes Bjerva, University of Copenhagen
Shuly Wintner, University of Haifa
Giuseppe Celano, Leipzig University
John Mansfield, University of Melbourne
Robert Östling, Stockholm University
Jörg Tiedemann , University of Helsinki
Željko Agić, Corti
Daan van Esch, Google AI
Tanja Samardžić, University of Zurich
Ella Rabinovich, University of Toronto
Barend Beekhuizen, University of Toronto
Nidhi Vyas, Carnegie Mellon University
Kilian Evang, University of Düsseldorf
Emily Ahn, Carnegie Mellon University
Annebeth Buis, The University of Colorado
Giulia Venturi, ILC "Antonio Zampolli"
Ada Wan, University of Zurich
Mark Ellison, Australian National University
Richard Futrell, University of California, Irvine
Michael Regan, University of New Mexico
Elisabetta Ježek, University of Pavia
Kyle Gorman, City University of New York
Joakim Nivre, Uppsala University
Chris Dyer, DeepMind
Emily Bender, University of Washington
Silvia Luraghi, Università di Pavia
Ehsan Asgari, UC Berkeley
Eleanor Chodroff, University of York
Elizabeth Salesky, Johns Hopkins University

Sabrina Mielke, Johns Hopkins University
Georgia Loukatou, Ecole Normale Supérieure

Invited Speakers:

Miriam Butt, University of Konstanz
Yulia Tsvetkov, Carnegie Mellon University
Richard Sproat, Google
Bill Croft, University of New Mexico
Harald Hammarström, Uppsala University

Table of Contents

Conference Program

Thursday, November 19, 2020

8:30–8:40 **Opening Session**

8:40–10:20 **Keynote Session 1**

8:40–9:30 *Invited Talk*
Richard Sproat

9:30–10:20 *Invited Talk*
Miriam Butt

10:20–10:30 **Coffee Break**

10:30–11:35 **Shared Task Session**

10:30–10:45 *SIGTYP 2020 Shared Task: Prediction of Typological Features*
Johannes Bjerva, Elizabeth Salesky, Sabrina J. Mielke, Aditi Chaudhary, Celano Giuseppe, Edoardo Maria Ponti, Ekaterina Vylomova, Ryan Cotterell and Isabelle Augenstein

10:45–10:55 *KMI-Panlingua-IITKGP @SIGTYP2020: Exploring rules and hybrid systems for automatic prediction of typological features*
Ritesh Kumar, Deepak Alok, Akanksha Bansal, Bornini Lahiri and Atul Kr. Ojha

10:55–11:05 *NEMO: Frequentist Inference Approach to Constrained Linguistic Typology Feature Prediction in SIGTYP 2020 Shared Task*
Alexander Gutkin and Richard Sproat

11:05–11:15 *Predicting Typological Features in WALS using Language Embeddings and Conditional Probabilities: ÚFAL Submission to the SIGTYP 2020 Shared Task*
Martin Vastl, Daniel Zeman and Rudolf Rosa

11:15–11:25 *Imputing typological values via phylogenetic inference*
Gerhard Jäger

11:25–11:35 *NUIG: Multitasking Self-attention based approach to SigTyp 2020 Shared Task*
Chinmay Choudhary

Thursday, November 19, 2020 (continued)

11:40–12:30 Keynote Session 2

11:40–12:30 *Invited Talk*
Harald Hammarström

12:20–12:30 Coffee Break

12:30–13:30 Oral Session 1

12:30–12:40 *DEmA: the Pavia Diachronic Emergence of Alignment database*
Sonia Cristofaro and Guglielmo Inglese

12:40–12:50 *A dataset and metric to evaluate lexical extraction from parallel corpora*
Barend Beekhuizen

12:50–13:00 *Keyword Spotting: A quick-and-dirty method for extracting typological features of language from grammatical descriptions*
Harald Hammarström

13:00–13:10 *SNACS Annotation of Case Markers and Adpositions in Hindi*
Aryaman Arora and Nathan Schneider

13:10–13:20 *Information from Topic Contexts: The Prediction of Aspectual Coding of Verbs in Russian*
Michael Richter and Tariq Yousef

13:20–13:30 *The role of community size and network structure in shaping linguistic diversity: experimental evidence*
Limor Raviv, Antje Mayer and Shiri Lev-Ari

Thursday, November 19, 2020 (continued)

13:30–14:05 Lunch Break

14:05–14:30 Findings Session 1

14:05–14:20 *SimAlign: High Quality Word Alignments without Parallel Training Data using Static and Contextualized Embeddings*
Masoud Jalili Sabet, Philipp Dufter, François Yvon and Hinrich Schütze

14:20–14:30 *Parsing with Multilingual BERT, a Small Corpus, and a Small Treebank*
Ethan C. Chau, Lucy H. Lin and Noah A. Smith

14:30–15:30 Oral Session 2

14:30–14:45 *Is Typology-Based Adaptation Effective for Multilingual Sequence Labelling?*
Ahmet Üstün, Arianna Bisazza, Gosse Bouma and Gertjan van Noord

14:45–15:00 *Multilingual BERT Learns Abstract Case Representations*
Isabel Papadimitriou, Ethan A. Chi, Richard Futrell and Kyle Mahowald

15:00–15:10 *Towards Induction of Structured Phoneme Inventories*
Alexander Gutkin, Martin Jansche and Lucy Skidmore

15:10–15:20 *Uncovering Typological Context-Sensitive Features*
Chiara Alzetta, Felice Dell'Orletta, Simonetta Montemagni and Giulia Venturi

15:20–15:30 *Multilingual Jointly Trained Acoustic and Written Word Embeddings*
Yushi Hu, Shane Settle and Karen Livescu

15:30–15:45 Findings Session 2

15:30–15:45 *Cross-lingual Alignment Methods for Multilingual BERT: A Comparative Study*
Saurabh Kulshreshtha, José Luis Redondo García and Ching-Yun Chang

15:45–16:20 Afternoon Break

16:20–18:00 Keynote Session 3

16:20–17:10 *Invited Talk*
Yulia Tsvetkov

17:10–18:00 *Invited Talk*
Bill Croft

18:00–18:10 Closing Session

Non-archival Abstracts

Information from topic contexts: the prediction of aspectual coding of verbs in Russian
Michael Richter and Tariq Yousef
Based on Shannon's coding theorem, we predict that aspectual coding asymmetries of verbs in Russian can be predicted by the verbal feature Average Information Content. We employ the novel Topic Context Model that calculates the verbal information content from the number of topics in the target words' larger discourses and their local discourses. In contrast to a previous study, TCM yielded disappointing results in this study which is, as we conclude, mainly due to the small number of local contexts we utilized.

Uncovering Typological Context-Sensitive Features
Chiara Alzetta, Felice Dell'Orletta, Simonetta Montemagni and Giulia Venturi
This contribution presents the results of a method for typological feature identification in multilingual treebanks. The results are exemplified on Italian and English subject relations. Applications of the method for multilingual dependency parsing evaluation are discussed.

Towards Induction of Structured Phoneme Inventories
Alexander Gutkin, Martin Jansche and Lucy Skidmore
This extended abstract provides a summary of our past and ongoing work on assessing the quality of multilingual phoneme inventories derived from typological resources, inducing phonological inventories using distinctive feature representations from the speech data and the important role phonological typology plays in these approaches.

Is Typology-Based Adaptation Effective for Multilingual Sequence Labelling?
Ahmet Üstün, Arianna Bisazza, Gosse Bouma and Gertjan van Noord
Recent work has shown that a single multilingual model with typologically informed parameter sharing can improve the performance in dependency parsing on both high-resource and zero-shot conditions. In this work, we investigate whether such improvements are also observed in the POS, NER and morphological tagging tasks.

SNACS Annotation of Case Markers and Adpositions in Hindi
Aryaman Arora and Nathan Schneider
The use of specific case markers and adpositions for particular semantic roles is idiosyncratic to every language. This poses problems in many natural language processing tasks such as machine translation and semantic role labelling. Models for these tasks rely on human-annotated corpora as training data.

There is a lack of corpora in South Asian languages for such tasks. Even Hindi, despite being a resource-rich language, is limited in available labelled data. This extended abstract presents the in-progress annotation of case markers and adpositions in a Hindi corpus, employing the cross-lingual scheme proposed by Schneider et al. (2017), Semantic Network of Adposition and Case Supersenses (SNACS). The SNACS guidelines we developed also apply to Urdu. We hope to finalize this corpus and develop NLP tools making use of the dataset, as well as promote NLP for typologically similar South Asian languages.

Multilingual Jointly Trained Acoustic and Written Word Embeddings
Yushi Hu, Shane Settle and Karen Livescu
Acoustic word embeddings (AWEs) are vector representations of spoken word segments. AWEs can be learned jointly with embeddings of character sequences, to generate phonetically meaningful embeddings of written words, or acoustically grounded word embeddings (AGWEs). Such embeddings have been used to improve speech retrieval, recognition, and spoken term discovery. In this work, we extend this idea to multiple low-resource languages. We jointly train an AWE model and an AGWE model, using phonetically transcribed data from multiple languages. The pre-trained models can then be used for unseen zero-resource languages, or fine-tuned on data from low-resource languages. We also investigate distinctive features, as an alternative to phone labels, to better share cross-lingual information. We test our models on word discrimination tasks for twelve languages while varying the amount of target language training data, and find significant benefits to the proposed multilingual approach.

Multilingual BERT learns abstract case representations
Isabel Papadimitriou, Ethan A. Chi, Richard Futrell and Kyle Mahowald
We investigate how Multilingual BERT (mBERT) encodes grammar by examining how the high-order grammatical feature of morphosyntactic alignment (how different languages define what counts as a "subject") is manifested across the embedding spaces of different languages. To understand if and how morphosyntactic alignment affects contextual embedding spaces, we train classifiers to recover the subjecthood of mBERT embeddings in transitive sentences (which do not contain overt information about morphosyntactic alignment) and then evaluate them zero-shot on intransitive sentences (where subjecthood classification depends on alignment), within and across languages. We find that the resulting classifier distributions reflect the morphosyntactic alignment of their training languages. Our results demonstrate that mBERT representations are influenced by high-level grammatical features that are not manifested in any one input sentence, and that this is robust across languages. Further examining the characteristics that our classifiers rely on, we find that features such as passive voice, animacy and case strongly correlate with classification decisions, suggesting that mBERT does not encode a purely syntactic subjecthood, but a continuous subjecthood as is proposed in much of the functional linguistics literature. Together, these results provide insight into how grammatical features manifest in contextual embedding spaces, at a level of abstraction not covered by previous work.

Keyword Spotting: A quick-and-dirty method for extracting typological features of language from grammatical descriptions
Harald Hammarström

DEmA: the Pavia Diachronic Emergence of Alignment database
Sonia Cristofaro and Guglielmo Inglese
This paper describes a workflow to impute missing values in a typological database, a subset of the World Atlas of Language Structures (WALS). Using a world-wide phylogeny derived from lexical data, the model assumes a phylogenetic continuous time Markov chain governing the evolution of typological values. Data imputation is performed via a Maximum Likelihood estimation on the basis of this model. As back-off model for languages whose phylogenetic position is unknown, a k-nearest neighbor classification based on geographic distance is performed.

A dataset and metric to evaluate lexical extraction from parallel corpora
Barend Beekhuizen
This work presents a novel dataset and a metric for evaluating methods for automated extraction of translation equivalent expressions in massively parallel corpora for the purposes of lexical semantic typology. Patterns in the annotation and the evaluation of the extraction methods were discussed, and directions for future research were indicated.

The role of community size and network structure in shaping linguistic diversity: experimental evidence
Limor Raviv, Antje Mayer and Shiri Lev-Ari
Why are there so many different languages in the world? How much do languages differ from each other in terms of their linguistic structure? And how do such differences come about?

One possibility is that linguistic diversity stems from differences in the social environments in which languages evolve. Specifically, it has been suggested that small, tightly knit communities can maintain high levels of linguistic complexity, while bigger and sparser communities tend to have languages that are structurally simpler, i.e., languages with more regular and more systematic grammars. However, to date this hypothesis has not been tested experimentally. Moreover, community size and network structure are typically confounded in the real-world, making it hard to evaluate the unique contribution of each social factor to this pattern of variation.

To address this issue, we used a novel group communication paradigm. This experimental paradigm allowed us to look at the live formation of new languages that were created in the lab by different micro-societies under different social conditions. By analyzing the emerging languages, we could tease apart the causal role of community size and network structure, and see how the process of language evolution and change is shaped by the fact that languages develop in communities of different sizes and different social structures.

During the group communication game, participants' goal was to communicate successfully about different novel scenes, using only invented nonsense words. A 'speaker' would see one of four shapes moving in some direction on a screen, and would type in a nonsense word to describe the scene (its shape and direction). The 'listener' would then guess which scene their partner was referring to by selecting one of eight scenes on their own screen. Participants received points for every successful interaction (correct guesses), and also feedback to allow them to learn for future interactions. Participants paired up with a different person from their group at every new round, taking turns producing and guessing words.

At the start of the game, people would randomly guessed meanings and make up new names. Over the course of several hours, participants started to combine words or part-words systematically, creating an actual mini-language. For instance, in one group, 'wowo-ik' meant that a specific shape was going up and right, whereas 'wowo-ii' meant that the same shape was going straight up. With such a 'regular' system, it becomes easier to predict the meaning of new labels ('mop-ik' meant a different shape going up and right).

In the first experiment, we examined the role of community size by having participants play in either 'small' groups of four participants or 'large' groups of eight participants. Would the large groups invent more structured languages than the small groups? Results showed that larger groups created languages with more systematic grammars, and did so faster and more consistently than small groups. This finding suggested that the number of people in the community can affect the grammar of languages. We suggest that larger groups are under a stronger pressure to create systematic languages because members of larger groups are typically faced with more input variability, and have less shared history with each member of their group.

In contrast, in the second experiment we found no evidence for a similar role of network structure. When we compared the performance of three network conditions (i.e., fully connected networks, small-world networks, scale-free networks) that varied in their degree of connectivity while group size constant was kept constant, we found that all groups developed languages that were highly systematic, communicatively efficient, stable, and shared across members, with dense and sparse groups reaching similar levels of linguistic structure over time. Although there were no significant differences between networks with respect to their degree of systematic grammar, we found that small-world networks showed the most variance in their behaviors. This result suggests that small-world networks may be more sensitive to random events (i.e., drift).

Together, the findings from the two experiments reported above show that factors in the social environment, and specifically community size, can affect patterns of language diversity and shape the nature and structure of languages.

SIGTYP 2020 Shared Task: Prediction of Typological Features

Johannes Bjerva[•,◁] **Elizabeth Salesky**[◇] **Sabrina J. Mielke**[◇] **Aditi Chaudhary**[□]
Giuseppe G. A. Celano[⊙] **Edoardo M. Ponti**[‡] **Ekaterina Vylomova**[♯]
Ryan Cotterell[⋆] **Isabelle Augenstein**[◁]
[•]Aalborg University [◁]University of Copenhagen [◇]Johns Hopkins University
[♯]University of Melbourne [□]Carnegie Mellon University [⊙]Leipzig University
[⋆]ETH Zürich [‡]University of Cambridge
jbjerva@cs.aau.dk, augenstein@di.ku.dk

Abstract

Typological knowledge bases (KBs) such as WALS (Dryer and Haspelmath, 2013) contain information about linguistic properties of the world's languages. They have been shown to be useful for downstream applications, including cross-lingual transfer learning and linguistic probing. A major drawback hampering broader adoption of typological KBs is that they are sparsely populated, in the sense that most languages only have annotations for some features, and skewed, in that few features have wide coverage. As typological features often correlate with one another, it is possible to predict them and thus automatically populate typological KBs, which is also the focus of this shared task. Overall, the task attracted 8 submissions from 5 teams, out of which the most successful methods make use of such feature correlations. However, our error analysis reveals that even the strongest submitted systems struggle with predicting feature values for languages where few features are known.

1 Introduction

Linguistic typology is the study of structural properties of languages (Comrie, 1988; Croft, 2002; Velupillai, 2012). Approaches to the categorisation of the languages of the world according to their linguistic properties are represented by, e.g., typological features in databases such as WALS (Dryer and Haspelmath, 2013), URIEL (Littell et al., 2017), and AUTOTYP (Nichols et al., 2013), e.g. in terms of their syntax, morphology, and phonology. One example of such a typological feature is the basic word order feature in WALS. For instance, English is best described as a subject-verb-object (SVO) language, whereas Japanese is best described as a subject-object-verb (SOV) language.

Once a relatively niche topic in the NLP community, studying typological features has recently risen in popularity and importance for a number of reasons. The field has seen considerable advances in cross-lingual transfer learning, whereby stable cross-lingual representations can be learned on massive amounts of data in an unsupervised way, be it for words (Ammar et al., 2016; Wada et al., 2019) or, more recently, sentences (Artetxe and Schwenk, 2019; Devlin et al., 2019; Conneau and Lample, 2019; Conneau et al., 2020). This naturally raises the question of what these representations encode, and some have turned to typology for potential answers (Choenni and Shutova, 2020; Zhao et al., 2020). In a similar vein, research has shown that these learned representations can be fine-tuned for supervised tasks, then applied to new languages in a few- or even zero-shot fashion with surprisingly high performance. This has raised the question of what causes such surprisingly high results, and to what degree typological similarities are exploited by such models (Bjerva and Augenstein, 2018a; Nooralahzadeh et al., 2020; Zhao et al., 2020).

In addition to using typology for diagnostic purposes, prior work has also found that typology can guide cross-lingual sharing (de Lhoneux et al., 2018). Finally, the relationship between typological knowledge bases (KBs) such as WALS (Dryer and Haspelmath, 2013) and language representations has been studied, which has shown that knowledge base population methods can be used to complete typological KBs (Malaviya et al., 2017; Murawaki, 2017; Bjerva and Augenstein, 2018a; Bjerva et al., 2019c), and that implications can be discovered in typological KBs (Daumé III and Campbell, 2007; Bjerva et al., 2019b).

The latter stream of work has provided the inspiration for this shared task on typological feature prediction. As knowledge bases are notoriously incomplete and require manual labour from (in this case, linguistic) domain experts to create, populate and maintain, high-performance methods for auto-

Proceedings of the Second Workshop on Computational Research in Linguistic Typology, pages 1–11
Online, November 19, 2020.

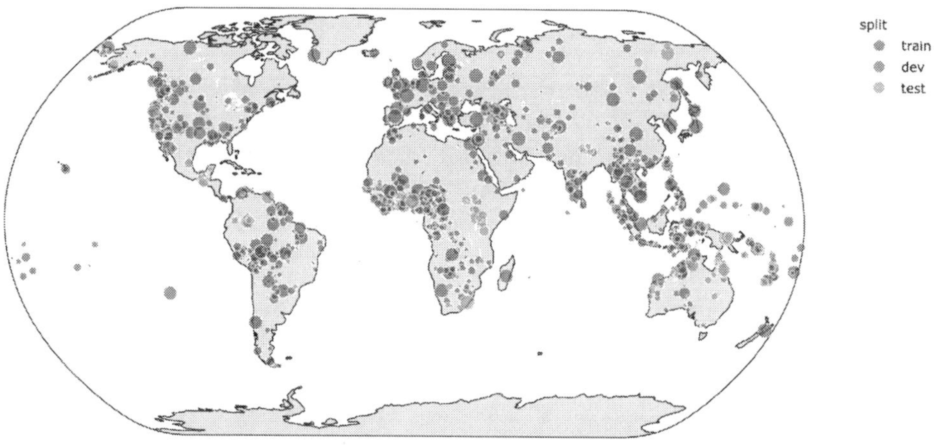

Figure 1: Shared task WALS data superimposed on a map showing one point per language with train, dev, and test splits; relative point sizes representing number of features for that language.

matic knowledge base population are highly desirable. While past approaches have shown the feasibility of typological feature prediction, the considered evaluation setups have some flaws which led to overestimated performance. Some papers control for phylogenetic relationships between languages, e.g. not both training and testing on Slavic languages, but little-to-no work has considered controlling for geographical proximity. This is corrected for in this shared task.

The shared task attracted 8 system submissions from 5 teams for two subtasks (constrained and unconstrained resources). In general, the systems which make use of correlations between features, and exploit observed features during inference, perform better, whereas those that do not make use of observed features perform similarly to our baselines.

2 Task Description

The SIGTYP 2020 shared task is concerned with predicting typological features from the World Atlas of Language Structures (WALS) (Dryer and Haspelmath, 2013). For the task, participants were invited to build systems to predict features for languages unseen at training time. The shared task consisted of two subtasks: 1) the *constrained* setting, for which only the provided training data may be used; 2) the *unconstrained* setting, for which training data may be extended with any external source of information (e.g. pre-trained embeddings, additional text, etc.)

Data Format For each instance, the following information is provided: the language code, name, latitude, longitude, genus, family, country code, and features. At training time, both the feature names and feature values are given, while at test time, submitted systems are required to fill values for the requested features. An example of a test instance is given in Table 1.

2.1 Dataset

WALS comprises 2679 languages and a total of 192 feature categories (Dryer and Haspelmath, 2013). However, the database is quite sparse in that many language-feature combinations lack annotation. Furthermore, it is a skewed database, in that a handful of languages have annotations for a large number of features, and some features are annotated for almost all languages, whereas some have very little coverage. In order to alleviate data sparsity in the shared task, only the subset of the languages in WALS with more than 3 features available are considered. Furthermore, of all the features of the languages so selected only those present in more than 9 languages have been retained. Most feature categories in WALS can take several feature values. For instance, the feature `Tone` can take one of the values: `No tones`, `Simple tone system`, or `Complex tone system`. This dataset has been divided into train set (90%), dev set (5%), and test set (5%).

	Lang code	Name	Lat	Long	Genus	Family	Count Code	Features
Input	mhi	Marathi	19.0	76.0	Indic	Indo-European	IN	order_of_subject,_object,_and_verb=? | number_of_genders=?
	jpn	Japanese	37.0	140.0	Japanese	Japanese	JP	case_syncretism=? | order_of_adjective_and_noun=?
Output	mhi	Marathi	19.0	76.0	Indic	Indo-European	IN	order_of_subject,_object,_and_verb=SOV | number_of_genders=three
	jpn	Japanese	37.0	140.0	Japanese	Japanese	JP	case_syncretism=no_case_marking | order_of_adjective_and_noun=demonstrative-Noun

Table 1: Data format for two test instances of the SIGTYP 2020 shared task dataset

3 Evaluation Setup

While a substantial amount of previous work deals with feature prediction in typological databases such as WALS (e.g. Malaviya et al. (2017); Murawaki (2017); Bjerva and Augenstein (2018a); Bjerva et al. (2019c)), most such work does not take into account that both phylogenetic and geographic proximity should be controlled for. Languages which have shared common ancestry will often have similar typological features, hence training and evaluating on the same language family will tend to inflate the expected performance of the model (Bjerva et al., 2019a). In the data for this shared task, we make sure to control for both of these factors.

Our evaluation setup is constructed as follows. We evaluate on a set of languages from small languages spread across the world, as defined by the WALS macroareas: Mayan (North America), Tucanoan (South America), Madang (Papuanesia), Mahakiranti (Eurasia), Northern Pama-Nyungan (Australia), and Nilotic (Africa). In addition, we include a subset of languages spoken around the world, by randomly sampling 10% of the available data in WALS. This yields two evaluation set-ups: one in which we evaluate on unobserved languages, controlling for both phylogenetic and geographic relationships, and one in which we perform a random evaluation as is common in previous work.

The languages in the test data vary in the number of removed and present feature values so that the *blanking ratios* are spread uniformly between 5% and 95%. This will allow our analysis to investigate whether some approaches benefit from observing a large number of features and whether some are robust to situations where only a small number of features are observed (subsection 5.4).

In order to control for phylogenetic and geographic effects, we remove all languages from the same language genus as the aforementioned languages from the training set, as well as all languages which are spoken within 1,000km of any of these languages.[1] This reduces the number of languages in the training set to 1250. The task had participants run their systems on the partial feature information for our held-out languages and send us the outputs of their systems, i.e., the imputed features.

3.1 Evaluation Metrics

We report macro-averaged accuracies, meaning that we first compute the average accuracy for each language, i.e., the fraction of to be imputed features correctly predicted by the participant's system, then average these language accuracies within each language genus, and finally report the average of these genus accuracies to rank participants as well as all these accuracies for each language genus (Section 5) to see whether systems behave differently on different language families. We judge statistical significance using a non-parametric two-tailed paired permutation test with 5k samples each.

3.2 Baselines

We provide two baselines. The first is a simple lower-bound baseline based on observing feature frequencies in WALS (Baseline_frequency in Figure 2). For each unobserved feature in the test set, we predict the most frequent feature value from the training set.

The second uses the k-nearest neighbours (k-NN) algorithm with a simple feature set to predict each unobserved feature, with $k = 1$ (Baseline_knn-imputation in Figure 2). Each language is represented by a language vector ($\vec{l} \in \mathbb{R}^{64}$) trained as a part of a multilingual character-based language model (Östling and Tiedemann, 2017). During inference, for a language l and unobserved feature y, we find the nearest neighbour to $\vec{l}$ for which y has been observed, similar to Bjerva and Augenstein (2018a,b).

[1]Distances calculated with WALS language locations.

3.3 Submissions

We received eight submissions from five teams across the *constrained* and *unconstrained* subtasks, as described below.

ÚFAL (Vastl et al. (2020), Charles University) submitted a *constrained* system which ensembled two approaches: first, estimating the correlation of feature values within languages enables missing feature prediction, and second, using a neural network to predict whether feature values match a specific language after training one network with all provided WALS feature values and pre-computed language embeddings. By ensembling both using confidence scores, they were able to improve on each individual approach and produce the best accuracy of all constrained and unconstrained submissions.

CrossLingference (Jäger (2020), University of Tübingen) submitted an *unconstrained* system using inferred phylogenetic trees. These were built with Continuous Time Markov Processes using Swadesh lists from the Automated Similarity Judgment Project (ASJP), with k-nearest neighbour estimations based on geographic information as back-off for test set languages not in both Glottolog and ASJP. Ancestral state reconstruction allows the inference of features for ancestral states from the provided surface features (WALS), and similarly, for this year's shared task, unknown feature values for non-ancestral languages can be inferred individually by rerooting the tree to a related language.

NUIG (Choudhary (2020), NUI Galway) submitted a *constrained* system with independent classifiers to predict each WALS feature. The outputs of independent classifiers are then fed into a shared encoder with feed-forward and self-attention layers in order to make use of feature correlations. Their model does not use other known features for WALS feature prediction at inference time, relying only on the 5-dimensional inputs of longitude, latitude, genus, family, and country-code.

NEMO (Gutkin and Sproat (2020), Google London and Tokyo) submitted *constrained* systems which first computed probabilities of represented feature values across each language's genetic (genus and family), and areal (features from languages within a 2,500 kilometre radius, computed from provided latitude and longitude with the Haversine formula), and *implicational universals* or rather, priors for certain features given commonly associated feature-value pairs in the data.

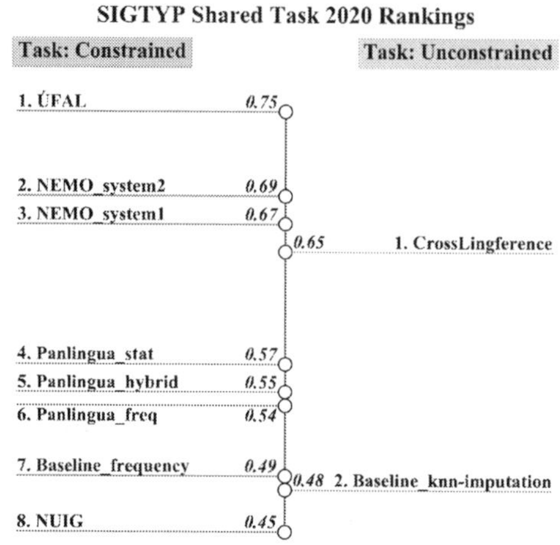

Figure 2: Macro-averaged rankings of all submissions

They compared several classifiers' performance using these sparse features, ultimately submitting systems using ridge regression. The two submitted systems differ in whether these features were computed for the test set or only train and dev.

Panlingua (Kumar et al., 2020), a team effort across KMI, Panlingua, and IIT KGP, submitted *constrained* systems from three approaches: two rule-based systems (one statistical, and one frequency-based baseline) and one hybrid system. Their baseline is similar to the organizers' frequency-base baseline, except that it produces the most frequent value for a feature within a genus if available, backing off to language family, and then the overall most-frequent value. The hybrid system uses 180 different SVM classifiers for the 180 features which were present in the training set. The statistical system provides a two-step back off procedure if neither a feature has been seen for either a languages' genus or family in training: first, finding the most frequent values in nearby languages using Haversine distance, and if these are too distant, turning to nearby language families. This system performed best on the held-out data.

4 Results

Figure 2 shows the overall results and rankings for all shared task submissions. The rankings use macro-averaged accuracies as this equally weights the controlled genera (the exception is the comparison to micro-averaged accuracies in Figure 3). This year's shared task was separated into two subtasks: *constrained* systems which used only the WALS

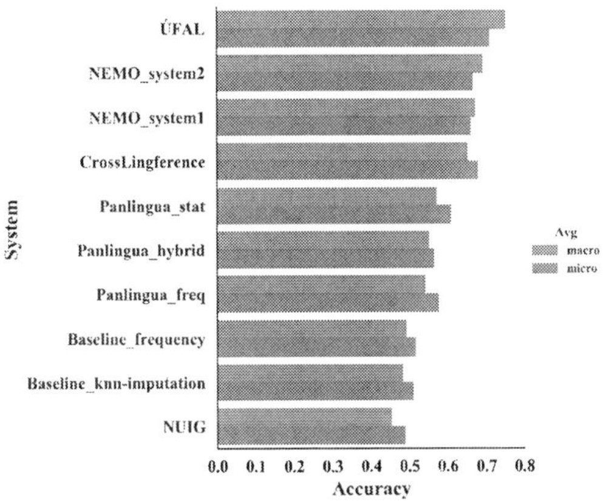

Figure 3: Comparison of macro-averaged and micro-averaged accuracies across submissions

features and data provided, and *unconstrained* systems, open to use of any data or pre-trained models. Accordingly, we have two winning systems: **ÚFAL** for *constrained*, and **CrossLingference** for *unconstrained*, with **ÚFAL** producing the best results overall across both subtasks.

Results for each unobserved genus, shown in comparison to results across genera observed in training, may be found in Table 2.

WALS feature value formatting is not standardized and, unfortunately, the test data was released containing additional tabs within the feature values for some features, which adversely affected teams who may have used tab-separation for data preprocessing. Many teams accounted for this and submitted feature values for all 2417 features across the 149 languages in the test data, but for two teams this led to missing features in their submissions: **CrossLingference** was missing 7 features across 7 languages, affecting their results by 1%; **Panlingua** was missing 61 features across 15 languages in their rule-based submission and 57 across 11 for their additional two submissions, affecting their results by 2%. When evaluating without the affected features, rankings were not changed, nor were there significant differences between submitted systems.

4.1 Subtask 1: Constrained Setting

The nine systems in the constrained setting used a diverse set of model features and architectures. When computing pairwise significances with a paired permutation test, we find that these systems cluster into three groups, within each the systems are not significantly different from each other: {**1**}, {**2-3**}, and {**4-8**}. Teams submitting multiple systems were able to improve their accuracy within their own submissions, but we did not find that their individual submissions were statistically significantly different. Similar differences in overall accuracy do not necessarily indicate statistically significant margins: for example, the 1st and 2nd systems have the same margin (0.05) as the 4th and 7th, but the latter are not significantly different while the former are.

Finer-grained analysis of results across controlled genera, and comparing results across different levels of representation in the training data, can be found in Section 5.

4.2 Subtask 2: Unconstrained Setting

CrossLingference submitted the only unconstrained system, which used additional data in the form of Swadesh lists to infer phylogenetic trees. This system outperforms the unconstrained knn-imputation baseline on all evaluated conditions. When we contextualize this submission by comparing it to those in the constrained setting, we find that it joins the second cluster with the two submissions from **NEMO**; interestingly, when features are micro-averaged rather than macro-averaged, these teams reorder, with **CrossLingference** outperforming the two **NEMO** systems, seen in Figure 3. This is somewhat counter-intuitive, given the way each system uses phylogenetic information. While **CrossLingference** explicitly models phylogenetic information through its model structure, **NEMO** takes a frequentist approach where the counts and probabilities of each feature within a language's genus, family, and geographic area are pre-computed and passed as sparse features to feature classifiers. One might expect the latter to perform better on a micro-average where overall data frequencies would be more heavily weighted than each genus, but this was not the case here. We explore this further in Section 5.

5 Analysis

Our test data was constructed to enable comparison across controlled phylogenetic and geographic relationships, and randomly sampled features from languages covered in training as is common in previous work.

Submission	Tucanoan (8)	Madang (9)	Mahakiranti (13)	Nilotic (15)	Mayan (17)	N. Pama-Nyungan (24)	Other genera (63)
ÚFAL	**0.73**	**0.78**	**0.74**	0.71	**0.80**	**0.76**	**0.76**
NEMO_system2	0.71	0.72	0.72	**0.76**	0.76	0.67	0.69
NEMO_system1	0.70	0.72	0.68	0.75	0.71	0.68	0.67
Panlingua_stat	0.70	0.64	0.55	0.55	0.33	0.62	0.58
Panlingua_hybrid	0.65	0.64	0.57	0.51	0.34	0.61	0.53
Panlingua_freq	0.59	0.64	0.53	0.55	0.31	0.59	0.55
Baseline_frequency	0.51	0.53	0.37	0.49	0.41	0.58	0.53
NUIG	0.51	0.56	0.35	0.45	0.32	0.45	0.48
CrossLingference	0.71	0.73	0.67	0.68	0.57	0.60	0.65
Baseline_knn-imputation	0.48	0.57	0.46	0.48	0.32	0.52	0.51

Table 2: Macro-averaged results across each unobserved genus, as compared to genera with languages observed in training with randomly sampled splits, shown with number of languages in each genus.

5.1 Overall Results

Table 2 compares submission accuracy on features from diverse WALS macroareas unobserved in training data, and other observed genera. We see that overall rankings hold when evaluated on observed languages. However, this is not the case for several of our unobserved genera. With respect to the shared task baselines, we find that the frequency baseline, which naively picks the most well-represented values for each feature, is most representative for the larger 'other genera' category, which represents the majority of the training data but does not account for the diversity of typological features and values across many languages. Nonetheless, for most of the unobserved genera, the frequency baseline performed better than the knn-imputation baseline, which was significantly better for Mahakiranti only, primarily due to correct prediction of "OV" ordering across multiple features.

Interestingly, while the first 3 systems perform better on macro-averaged accuracy than micro-averaged (Figure 3), this is not true for all other systems, suggesting that they rely more on getting frequent and "easy" features right, relying on frequency in training data. Note that the six unobserved genera come from separate macroareas across six different continents, and have a more even distribution of feature values than the 'other genera.'

5.2 Differences across Genera

Looking at specific genera, we see that Mayan caused the greatest split between submitted systems, with the first two clusters performing very well, and the frequency baseline performed better than the majority of systems. On the other end of the spectrum, certain genera (Tucanoan and Madang) with well-represented features were relative equalizers, with the least variance in results across the submitted systems.

Within those teams which submitted multiple systems, there were only certain cases in which these performed significantly differently from each other. **Panlingua** submitted three different systems; two rule-based (one statistical and one frequency-based), and one hybrid model. For most genera, these performed very similarly, with consistently better results from the statistical rule-based system than the others, though there were no statistically significant differences shown by paired permutation tests. However, this was not the case for Tucanoan, where the statistical (and to a less degree, hybrid) model significantly outperformed the other. These systems had equal performance on four of the Tucanoan languages {Cubeo,Secoya,Siona,Koreguaje}, but quite divergent on the remaining four languages {Desano,Retuarã,Tucano,Tuyuca}. This second set required predicting values for several features concerning the order of Subject, Object, Verb, which the statistical model was able to correctly predict through better back-off choices, but swayed by the more frequent SVO languages in training, their frequency baseline and SVM-based classifiers were not.

5.3 Differences among Features

Table 3 shows the features with the highest and lowest accuracies across all submissions. We find that the features with highest accuracies also have the most consistent performance across all systems, and typically have the most frequent values for

	Feature	# Langs	Avg. Accuracy	Std. Deviation
Highest	front_rounded_vowels	4	0.65	0.08
	inclusive/exclusive_forms_in_pama-nyungan	2	0.65	0.09
	distributive_numerals	3	0.64	0.08
	optional_double_negation_in_svo_languages	1	0.64	0.08
	voicing_in_plosives_and_fricatives	4	0.63	0.08
Lowest	verb-initial_with_clause-final_negative	1	0.44	0.21
	multiple_negative_constructions_in_svo_languages	3	0.41	0.27
	suppletion_in_imperatives_and_hortatives	2	0.40	0.13
	languages_with_two_dominant_orders_of_subject,_object,_and_verb	2	0.39	0.20
	the_position_of_negative_morphemes_in_verb-initial_languages	9	0.38	0.28

Table 3: Features with the highest and lowest overall accuracies across *all* submissions, with number of languages containing the feature in the test data (183 total languages)

those features. The most difficult features, on the other hand, have the least frequently occurring values in the training data, and have higher variance – interestingly, the top four systems were nonetheless able to achieve greater than 65% accuracy on these features, while the remaining systems' accuracies were $\sim 20\%$.

5.4 Impact of Blanking Ratio

Since the languages in our test sets all remove and retain different numbers of features, we can see whether the blanking ratio, that is, the ratio of features that participants have to impute to the features listed for that language, correlates with the performance of the system in question on that language. Calculating Pearson's correlation coefficient for every system individually, we realize that they range from -0.23 (for a NEMO system) to 0.31 (for a Panlingua system), almost all of which statistically significantly different from 0.

Why do these correlations differ so much from system to system? To answer that question, we plot these correlation coefficients as a function of the system's overall performance in Figure 4. It turns out that a system's overall performance and how sensitive it is to the blanking ratio are highly correlated: the stronger systems are much more negatively affected by the removal of more features (their correlations are negative), weaker systems are not only not harmed, but seem to find the languages where only a few features are blanked harder still (having positive correlations).

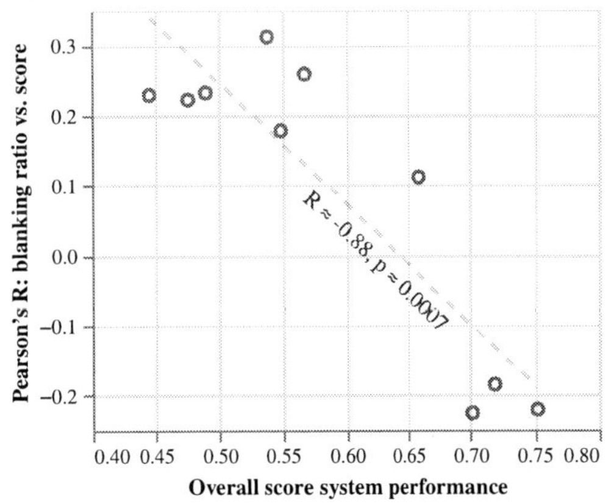

Figure 4: Correlation coefficients (between blanking ratio and language performance) for each system as a function of that system's performance. The correlation of $\text{R} = -0.88$ is significant at $p < .001$.

6 Related Work

Previous work can be divided into research on predicting typological features automatically, cross-lingual transfer learning which utilises typology to inform sharing, probing of representations for what typological knowledge they encode, and finally, work on how best to represent a language in terms of its typological features.

6.1 Predicting Typological Features

Typological knowledge bases are both sparse and skewed in terms of language–feature annotations. They are sparse in the sense that most languages only have annotations for a handful of features and skewed in the sense that a few features have much wider coverage than others. Luckily, such features often correlate with one another, which allows for prediction of those features from others. For instance, languages where the verb precedes the object tend to have prepositions, e.g. Norwegian, whereas languages where the object precedes the verb word tend to have postpositions, e.g. Japanese.

A survey of approaches to prediction of features

is provided in Ponti et al. (2019a, § 4.3). Some common approaches include prediction based on language representations learned as a by-product of model training (Östling and Tiedemann, 2017; Malaviya et al., 2017; Bjerva and Augenstein, 2018a; Bjerva et al., 2019c) and matrix factorisation (Murawaki, 2017; Bjerva et al., 2019a).

6.2 Typologically Informed Sharing

Cross-lingual sharing informed by typology has been investigated for, among others, parsing (Naseem et al., 2012; Täckström et al., 2013; Zhang and Barzilay, 2015; de Lhoneux et al., 2018), language modeling (Tsvetkov et al., 2016; Ponti et al., 2019b), machine translation (Daiber et al., 2016; Ponti et al., 2018), and morphological inflection (Chaudhary et al., 2019). Many of these approaches use language embeddings with sparse features encoding WALS feature values. Oncevay et al. (2020) find that combining information from typological databases with embeddings learned during training of an NMT model can be beneficial for multilingual NMT.

6.3 Typological Probing

Several recent papers study typological feature prediction as a probing task for evaluating cross-lingual sentence encoders (Choenni and Shutova, 2020; Bjerva and Augenstein, 2018a; Nooralahzadeh et al., 2020; Zhao et al., 2020). Typically, hidden representations are probed for whether or not they might encode a typological feature by, e.g., using them in a separate classifier (Malaviya et al., 2017; Bjerva and Augenstein, 2018a; Nooralahzadeh et al., 2020). Östling and Tiedemann (2017) learn language representations during multilingual language modelling and find that the resulting representations can reproduce relatively credible phylogenetic trees.

Bjerva and Augenstein (2018a) learn language representations under NLP tasks such as POS tagging and grapheme-to-phoneme conversion, and find that typological features related to the task at hand are sometimes encoded. Nooralahzadeh et al. (2020) use a typological probing task in experiments for zero- and few-shot NLI and QA, finding that languages which share typological properties benefit from sharing. Zhao et al. (2020) attempt to induce language-agnostic representations, e.g. by reducing the typological gaps between languages, and find that this is beneficial for NLI and MT. Gerz et al. (2018) show that there is a correlation between typological features related to morphology and model performance in language modelling, and Cotterell et al. (2018) further show that inflectional morphology affects performance in both n-gram and LSTM-based language models.

7 Conclusions

This paper documents the first SIGTYP shared task on prediction of typological features in WALS. The 8 system submissions from 5 teams showed that a variety of different methods can be applied to the task. Interestingly, the best system only achieved a macro-averaged accuracy of 75%, indicating that the task is far from solved. This further shows that the evaluation set-up in which we controlled for both phylogenetic relationships and geographic proximity is a challenging one. We expect that further exploration of unconstrained systems to have the most potential for predicting features in such cases, where little or nothing is known about a language.

Acknowledgments

This research has received funding from the Swedish Research Council under grant agreement No 2019-04129, as well as the German Research Foundation (DFG project number 408121292).

References

Waleed Ammar, George Mulcaire, Yulia Tsvetkov, Guillaume Lample, Chris Dyer, and Noah A. Smith. 2016. Massively Multilingual Word Embeddings. *CoRR*, abs/1602.01925.

Mikel Artetxe and Holger Schwenk. 2019. Massively Multilingual Sentence Embeddings for Zero-Shot Cross-Lingual Transfer and Beyond. *Trans. Assoc. Comput. Linguistics*, 7:597–610.

Johannes Bjerva and Isabelle Augenstein. 2018a. From phonology to syntax: Unsupervised linguistic typology at different levels with language embeddings. In *Proceedings of the 2018 Conference of the North American Chapter of the Association for Computational Linguistics: Human Language Technologies, Volume 1 (Long Papers)*, pages 907–916, New Orleans, Louisiana. Association for Computational Linguistics.

Johannes Bjerva and Isabelle Augenstein. 2018b. Tracking Typological Traits of Uralic Languages in Distributed Language Representations. In *Proceedings of the Fourth International Workshop on Computational Linguistics of Uralic Languages*, pages 76–86, Helsinki, Finland. Association for Computational Linguistics.

Johannes Bjerva, Yova Kementchedjhieva, Ryan Cotterell, and Isabelle Augenstein. 2019a. A probabilistic generative model of linguistic typology. In *Proceedings of the 2019 Conference of the North American Chapter of the Association for Computational Linguistics: Human Language Technologies, Volume 1 (Long and Short Papers)*, pages 1529–1540, Minneapolis, Minnesota. Association for Computational Linguistics.

Johannes Bjerva, Yova Kementchedjhieva, Ryan Cotterell, and Isabelle Augenstein. 2019b. Uncovering probabilistic implications in typological knowledge bases. In *Proceedings of the 57th Annual Meeting of the Association for Computational Linguistics*, pages 3924–3930, Florence, Italy. Association for Computational Linguistics.

Johannes Bjerva, Robert Östling, Maria Han Veiga, Jörg Tiedemann, and Isabelle Augenstein. 2019c. What do language representations really represent? *Computational Linguistics*, 45(2):381–389.

Aditi Chaudhary, Elizabeth Salesky, Gayatri Bhat, David R. Mortensen, Jaime Carbonell, and Yulia Tsvetkov. 2019. CMU-01 at the SIGMORPHON 2019 shared task on crosslinguality and context in morphology. In *Proceedings of the 16th Workshop on Computational Research in Phonetics, Phonology, and Morphology*, pages 57–70, Florence, Italy. Association for Computational Linguistics.

Rochelle Choenni and Ekaterina Shutova. 2020. What does it mean to be language-agnostic? probing multilingual sentence encoders for typological properties. *CoRR*, abs/2009.12862.

Chinmay Choudhary. 2020. NUIG: Multitasking Self-attention based approach to SigTyp 2020 Shared Task. In *Proceedings of the Second Workshop on Computational Research in Linguistic Typology*. Association for Computational Linguistics.

Bernard Comrie. 1988. Linguistic typology. *Annual Review of Anthropology*, 17:145–159.

Alexis Conneau, Kartikay Khandelwal, Naman Goyal, Vishrav Chaudhary, Guillaume Wenzek, Francisco Guzmán, Edouard Grave, Myle Ott, Luke Zettlemoyer, and Veselin Stoyanov. 2020. Unsupervised Cross-lingual Representation Learning at Scale. In *ACL*, pages 8440–8451. Association for Computational Linguistics.

Alexis Conneau and Guillaume Lample. 2019. Cross-lingual Language Model Pretraining. In *NeurIPS*, pages 7057–7067.

Ryan Cotterell, Sabrina J. Mielke, Jason Eisner, and Brian Roark. 2018. Are all languages equally hard to language-model? In *Proceedings of the 2018 Conference of the North American Chapter of the Association for Computational Linguistics: Human Language Technologies, Volume 2 (Short Papers)*, pages 536–541, New Orleans, Louisiana. Association for Computational Linguistics.

William Croft. 2002. *Typology and Universals*. Cambridge University Press.

Joachim Daiber, Miloš Stanojević, and Khalil Sima'an. 2016. Universal reordering via linguistic typology. In *Proceedings of COLING 2016, the 26th International Conference on Computational Linguistics: Technical Papers*, pages 3167–3176, Osaka, Japan. The COLING 2016 Organizing Committee.

Hal Daumé III and Lyle Campbell. 2007. A Bayesian Model for Discovering Typological Implications. In *Proceedings of the 45th Annual Meeting of the Association of Computational Linguistics*, pages 65–72, Prague, Czech Republic. Association for Computational Linguistics.

Jacob Devlin, Ming-Wei Chang, Kenton Lee, and Kristina Toutanova. 2019. BERT: Pre-training of Deep Bidirectional Transformers for Language Understanding. In *Proceedings of the 2019 Conference of the North American Chapter of the Association for Computational Linguistics: Human Language Technologies, Volume 1 (Long and Short Papers)*, pages 4171–4186, Minneapolis, Minnesota. Association for Computational Linguistics.

Matthew S. Dryer and Martin Haspelmath, editors. 2013. *WALS Online*. Max Planck Institute for Evolutionary Anthropology, Leipzig.

Daniela Gerz, Ivan Vulić, Edoardo Maria Ponti, Roi Reichart, and Anna Korhonen. 2018. On the relation between linguistic typology and (limitations of) multilingual language modeling. In *Proceedings of the 2018 Conference on Empirical Methods in Natural Language Processing*, pages 316–327, Brussels, Belgium. Association for Computational Linguistics.

Alexander Gutkin and Richard Sproat. 2020. NEMO: Frequentist Inference Approach to Constrained Linguistic Typology Feature Prediction in SIGTYP 2020 Shared Task. In *Proceedings of the Second Workshop on Computational Research in Linguistic Typology*. Association for Computational Linguistics.

Gerhard Jäger. 2020. Imputing typological values via phylogenetic inference. In *Proceedings of the Second Workshop on Computational Research in Linguistic Typology*. Association for Computational Linguistics.

Ritesh Kumar, Deepak Alok, Akanksha Bansal, Bornini Lahiri, and Atul Kr. Ojha. 2020. KMI-Panlingua-IITKGP at SIGTYP2020: Exploring rules and hybrid systems for automatic prediction of typological features. In *Proceedings of the Second Workshop on Computational Research in Linguistic Typology*. Association for Computational Linguistics.

Miryam de Lhoneux, Johannes Bjerva, Isabelle Augenstein, and Anders Søgaard. 2018. Parameter sharing between dependency parsers for related languages. In *Proceedings of the 2018 Conference on*

Empirical Methods in Natural Language Processing, pages 4992–4997, Brussels, Belgium. Association for Computational Linguistics.

Patrick Littell, David R. Mortensen, Ke Lin, Katherine Kairis, Carlisle Turner, and Lori Levin. 2017. Uriel and lang2vec: Representing languages as typological, geographical, and phylogenetic vectors. In *Proceedings of the 15th Conference of the European Chapter of the Association for Computational Linguistics: Volume 2, Short Papers*, pages 8–14. Association for Computational Linguistics.

Chaitanya Malaviya, Graham Neubig, and Patrick Littell. 2017. Learning language representations for typology prediction. In *Proceedings of the 2017 Conference on Empirical Methods in Natural Language Processing*, pages 2529–2535, Copenhagen, Denmark. Association for Computational Linguistics.

Yugo Murawaki. 2017. Diachrony-aware induction of binary latent representations from typological features. In *Proceedings of the Eighth International Joint Conference on Natural Language Processing (Volume 1: Long Papers)*, pages 451–461, Taipei, Taiwan. Asian Federation of Natural Language Processing.

Tahira Naseem, Regina Barzilay, and Amir Globerson. 2012. Selective sharing for multilingual dependency parsing. In *Proceedings of the 50th Annual Meeting of the Association for Computational Linguistics (Volume 1: Long Papers)*, pages 629–637, Jeju Island, Korea. Association for Computational Linguistics.

Johanna Nichols, Alena Witzlack-Makarevich, and Balthasar Bickel. 2013. The autotyp genealogy and geography database: 2013 release. *Zurich: University of Zurich.*

Farhad Nooralahzadeh, Giannis Bekoulis, Johannes Bjerva, and Isabelle Augenstein. 2020. Zero-Shot Cross-Lingual Transfer with Meta Learning. In *Proceedings of EMNLP*. Association for Computational Linguistics.

Arturo Oncevay, Barry Haddow, and Alexandra Birch. 2020. Bridging linguistic typology and multilingual machine translation with multi-view language representations. In *Proceedings of EMNLP*. Association for Computational Linguistics. ArXiv preprint arXiv:2004.14923.

Robert Östling and Jörg Tiedemann. 2017. Continuous multilinguality with language vectors. In *Proceedings of the 15th Conference of the European Chapter of the Association for Computational Linguistics: Volume 2, Short Papers*, pages 644–649, Valencia, Spain. Association for Computational Linguistics.

Edoardo Maria Ponti, Helen O'horan, Yevgeni Berzak, Ivan Vulić, Roi Reichart, Thierry Poibeau, Ekaterina Shutova, and Anna Korhonen. 2019a. Modeling language variation and universals: A survey on typological linguistics for natural language processing. *Computational Linguistics*, 45(3):559–601.

Edoardo Maria Ponti, Roi Reichart, Anna Korhonen, and Ivan Vulić. 2018. Isomorphic transfer of syntactic structures in cross-lingual NLP. In *Proceedings of the 56th Annual Meeting of the Association for Computational Linguistics (Volume 1: Long Papers)*, pages 1531–1542, Melbourne, Australia. Association for Computational Linguistics.

Edoardo Maria Ponti, Ivan Vulić, Ryan Cotterell, Roi Reichart, and Anna Korhonen. 2019b. Towards zero-shot language modeling. In *Proceedings of the 2019 Conference on Empirical Methods in Natural Language Processing and the 9th International Joint Conference on Natural Language Processing (EMNLP-IJCNLP)*, pages 2900–2910, Hong Kong, China. Association for Computational Linguistics.

Oscar Täckström, Ryan McDonald, and Joakim Nivre. 2013. Target language adaptation of discriminative transfer parsers. In *Proceedings of the 2013 Conference of the North American Chapter of the Association for Computational Linguistics: Human Language Technologies*, pages 1061–1071, Atlanta, Georgia. Association for Computational Linguistics.

Yulia Tsvetkov, Sunayana Sitaram, Manaal Faruqui, Guillaume Lample, Patrick Littell, David Mortensen, Alan W Black, Lori Levin, and Chris Dyer. 2016. Polyglot neural language models: A case study in cross-lingual phonetic representation learning. In *Proceedings of the 2016 Conference of the North American Chapter of the Association for Computational Linguistics: Human Language Technologies*, pages 1357–1366, San Diego, California. Association for Computational Linguistics.

Martin Vastl, Daniel Zeman, and Rudolf Rosa. 2020. Predicting Typological Features in WALS using Language Embeddings and Conditional Probabilities: ÚFAL Submission to the SIGTYP 2020 Shared Task. In *Proceedings of the Second Workshop on Computational Research in Linguistic Typology*. Association for Computational Linguistics.

Viveka Velupillai. 2012. *An introduction to linguistic typology*. John Benjamins Publishing Company Amsterdam, Philadelphia.

Takashi Wada, Tomoharu Iwata, and Yuji Matsumoto. 2019. Unsupervised Multilingual Word Embedding with Limited Resources using Neural Language Models. In *ACL (1)*, pages 3113–3124. Association for Computational Linguistics.

Yuan Zhang and Regina Barzilay. 2015. Hierarchical low-rank tensors for multilingual transfer parsing. In *Proceedings of the 2015 Conference on Empirical Methods in Natural Language Processing*, pages 1857–1867, Lisbon, Portugal. Association for Computational Linguistics.

Wei Zhao, Steffen Eger, Johannes Bjerva, and Isabelle Augenstein. 2020. Inducing Language-Agnostic Multilingual Representations. *arXiv preprint arXiv:2008.09112*.

KMI-Panlingua-IITKGP @SIGTYP2020: Exploring Rules and Hybrid Systems for Automatic Prediction of Typological Features

Ritesh Kumar[1], Deepak Alok[2], Akanksha Bansal[3],
Bornini Lahiri[4], Atul Kr. Ojha[5,3],
[1]Dr. Bhimrao Ambedkar University, Agra, [2]Rutgers University, USA,
[5]NUIG, Galway, [3]Panlingua Language Processing LLP, New Delhi,
[4]Indian Institute of Technology, Kharagpur,
ritesh78_llh@jnu.ac.in, bornini@hss.iitkgp.ac.in
(deepak06alok, akanksha.bansal15, shashwatup9k)@gmail.com

Abstract

This paper enumerates SigTyP 2020 Shared Task on the prediction of typological features as performed by the KMI-Panlingua-IITKGP team. The task entailed the prediction of missing values in a particular language, provided, the name of the language family, its genus, location (in terms of latitude and longitude coordinates and name of the country where it is spoken) and a set of feature-value pair are available. As part of fulfillment of the aforementioned task, the team submitted 3 kinds of system - 2 rule-based and one hybrid system. Of these 3, one rule-based system generated the best performance on the test set. All the systems were 'constrained' in the sense that no additional dataset or information, other than those provided by the organisers, was used for developing the systems.

1 Introduction

This paper is a detailed documentation of the KMI-Panlingua-IITKGP team's system submission at the SigTyP 2020 Shared Task on the prediction of typological features. The objective behind this task is to develop a computational model that predicts (missing) linguistic features of a language, given its location, language family, genus, and a set of feature-value pair. The shared task organisers provided the dataset used for this purpose, which has been extracted from Worlds Atlas of Language structures (WALS) (see section 2 for details). Since the provided dataset was not large and comprised of unevenly distributed features, we prepared and experimented with three different systems and compare them with each other to provide the best model. Of these three systems, 2 are rule-based, in which, one is frequency-based system (see subsection 3.1) and the other is statistical system (see subsection 3.2). The third one is a hybrid (see subsection 3.3). The statistical system provides the best results among the three (see section 4). This paper promises two major contributions. First, it provides an automatic system that enables extraction of feature-value pair of a given language - a tedious job if done manually. Second, it compares three different systems and provides evidence that a statistical model gives better results for the given data set.

2 Dataset

The dataset[1] used for this experiment was extracted from World Atlas of Language Structures (WALS) (Dryer and Haspelmath, 2013). It covered the typological features of close to 2,000 languages (Bjerva et al., 2020). These typological features were organised in 8 columns (including Language ID, Language name, Latitude, Longitude, Genus, Family, Country

[1]https://github.com/sigtyp/ST2020/tree/master/data

Proceedings of the Second Workshop on Computational Research in Linguistic Typology, pages 12–16
Online, November 19, 2020.

Codes, and feature-value. The feature values were separated by '|' for each language). The task was divided into two sub-tasks: (a) Constrained and (b) Unconstrained. The dataset was sub-divided into training, dev, and test sets. Out of 1,125 training instances, Genus had 280 different features, Country had 258 different features, Family had 127 different features and Features had 185 different feature-values. Out of 84 dev instances, Genus had 50 different features, Country had 32, Family had 36, while Features had 182 different feature-values. Out of 149 test instances, Genus had 42 different features, Country had 30, Family had 35, while Features had 183 different feature-values (see Table 1).

	Genus	Family	Country	Features
Training	280	127	258	185
Dev	50	36	32	182
Test	42	35	30	183

Table 1: Statistics of the dataset at Genus, Family, Country and Features

3 Experiments

Our task consisted of 3 experiments and this section enumerates and discusses each one of the systems in detail. All the 3 systems are based on the notion of shared typological properties of languages belonging to the same language family (or sub-family, represented as genus in the dataset) and shared areal properties of languages belonging to different language families but being in regular contact by virtue of being in close contact, mainly because of speakers residing in close geographical proximity.

3.1 Baseline System

Our baseline system is a frequency-based system that makes use of the language family and genus-based typological properties to predict the grammatical features of a given language. In the training phase, for each feature, frequency of each of its value in each of the language family and genus is calculated and stored. During the prediction, for a specific feature in a given language (under the given language family and genus), the feature value with the maximum frequency within that genus (or language family, if the genus does not occur in the training data) is predicted as the value for the concerned feature. If neither the language family nor the genus occurs during the training phase then a default value of the feature is predicted by the system.

3.2 Statistical System

The statistical system is an extension of our baseline system where the absence of both the language family and the genus in the training data is handled in a more principled way. In such cases, we made use of the 'distance' between two languages to decide on the feature values. The training phase for this system is exactly the same as that of our baseline system. However, during prediction, the following steps are taken -

1. Step 1: As in the case of the baseline system, if the genus of the language whose feature is to be predicted is seen during the training phase and if the feature that is to be predicted was seen in that genus during the training phase then the value that was most frequent for that genus-feature combination is predicted as the value for the current case. In case the genus of the language or the concerned feature was not seen in the genus then the same step is carried out with the language family. If neither genus-feature nor family-feature combination is seen in the training phase then we move to Step 2.

2. Step 2: In the second step, based on the latitude and longitude position of the

given language, the Haversine distance between the language for which the feature value is to be predicted, and all the other languages in the training set, is calculated. Then we take the language families and genus of the four closest languages. We look at the frequency of each feature value across these four closest language families and the value with the maximum frequency is predicted as the correct feature value. The choice of four closest language families is established experimentally, by looking at numbers from 1 - 10 and deciding on the basis of best performance with the train set. If the feature is not found in these four closest language families then we move to step 3.

3. Step 3: In the third step, we look at the closest language family and genus which has the feature that we are trying to predict. The system takes the feature value with the maximum frequency and predict that, as the value for the feature. In this and the previous step, it is to be noted that each feature may have multiple values in a specific language family and genus - as such the value which occurs in the maximum number of languages of that family and genus is the one that is considered most frequent and, hence, predicted.

3.3 Hybrid System

For the hybrid system, we trained 180 different classifiers for the 180 features, which were present in the training set. Since it was not a huge dataset, with quite uneven distribution of each features and the features for training were also limited, we used SVM (Pedregosa et al., 2011), (Buitinck et al., 2013) for training each of the classifier. We experimented with different c-values from 0.001 - 10. For each feature, there were 1,100 training data points (each data point for each language in the dataset). We used the normalised Haversine distance (calculated using the coordinates), language family, genus, country and the other 179 linguistic features as features for training the classifiers. All the features not listed for a specific language was considered absent in that language; otherwise its assigned value was used for training. As mentioned earlier, since the dataset was imbalanced and some features were adequately represented while others occurred only a few times in the dataset, the performance of the classifiers accordingly varied from approx 0.30 - 0.98 (F-score). Clearly, it would not have been possible to use the classifiers that performed too low. As such we decided to use only those classifiers which had an F-score of 0.6 or above; for the other features, the statistical method (outlined in the previous section) was employed. This F-score was again experimentally deduced by looking at the best performance for multiple systems ranging from an all classifier-based system to using only those classifiers with 0.9 or above F1 score. The performance was measured by predicting features in the train set for different languages i.e. the train accuracy was taken as the benchmark for deciding this value.

4 Results

Among the three systems, our statistical system performed the best on the test set with a micro-average F-score (see Table 2) of slightly under 0.61 (a 10-point gain over the knn-imputation baseline, 9 point gain over the frequency-based baseline). The hybrid system performed the worst among the three systems with a score of slightly above 0.56.

While we were expecting the hybrid system to work better than the statistical system (since we assumed that it combined the best of both worlds), in the final results, it is the statistical systems (even the most naive one) that perform better than the hybrid systems. This

Systems	Score
kmi-panlingua-iitkgp_constrained_rule	0.607
kmi-panlingua-iitkgp_constrained_hybrid	0.562
kmi-panlingua-iitkgp_constrained	0.574
frequency-baseline_constrained	0.513
knn-imputation-baseline_constrained	0.507

Table 2: Overall accuracy of the KMI-Panlingua-IITKGP Systems

shows that even in those cases where SVMs have performed reasonably well, the statistical systems have performed equally well or better than the SVMs. There are two takeaways from this -

- **Size of Datatset:** For some of the features (especially those 2 or 3 values), such as absence of common consonants' or 'number of possessive nouns', SVMs seems to perform quite well. However, other features such as 'Action Nominal Constructions', which have a high number of classes (9 in this case), there were just not sufficient instances of each class to get sufficient discriminating features for adequate classification. One way of handling this could be by looking at the correlation among features and giving higher weightage to the features that are more likely to co-occur with each other.

- **Typological and Areal Features:** The typological and areal features are derived via systematic study of multiple languages and prior linguistic studies have shown that language families as well as geographically closer languages share certain linguistic features. The statistical system makes use of these generalisations about human language and manages to capture, at least partially, these properties of human languages. This could be one of the reasons why the statistical system performs better than the hybrid system, where sufficient information was not available to the classifier to make this kind of generalisation. This also provides some kind of explicit validity to the arguments related to the use of typological and areal features for augmenting the NLP systems, especially in low-resource situations. In this case even with minimal data and a rather naive approach our statistical system has outperformed a SVM-based hybrid system - this itself attests the fact that typological and areal features capture a significant generalisation about human languages and they could prove to be very valuable, if used judiciously, for low-resource NLP.

5 Conclusion

In this paper, we presented two rule-based systems and one hybrid system to predict typological features of a given language. We demonstrated that the statistical, a rule-based system, gave the best performance on the test set. Only the data set provided by the organisers was used for developing the systems.

References

Johannes Bjerva, Elizabeth Salesky, Sabrina Mielke, Aditi Chaudhary, Giuseppe G. A. Celano, Edoardo M. Ponti, Ekaterina Vylomova, Ryan Cotterell, and Isabelle Augenstein. 2020. SIGTYP 2020 Shared Task: Prediction of Typological Features. In *Proceedings of the Second Workshop on Computational Research in Linguistic Typology*. Association for Computational Linguistics.

Lars Buitinck, Gilles Louppe, Mathieu Blondel, Fabian Pedregosa, Andreas Mueller, Olivier Grisel, Vlad Niculae, Peter Prettenhofer, Alexandre Gramfort, Jaques Grobler, Robert Layton, Jake VanderPlas, Arnaud Joly, Brian Holt, and Gaël Varoquaux. 2013. API design for machine learning software: experiences from the scikit-learn project. In *ECML PKDD Workshop: Languages for Data Mining and Machine Learning*, pages 108–122.

Matthew S. Dryer and Martin Haspelmath, editors. 2013. *WALS Online*. Max Planck Institute for Evolutionary Anthropology, Leipzig.

F. Pedregosa, G. Varoquaux, A. Gramfort, V. Michel, B. Thirion, O. Grisel, M. Blondel, P. Prettenhofer, R. Weiss, V. Dubourg, J. Vanderplas, A. Passos, D. Cournapeau, M. Brucher, M. Perrot, and E. Duchesnay. 2011. Scikit-learn: Machine learning in Python. *Journal of Machine Learning Research*, 12:2825–2830.

NEMO: Frequentist Inference Approach to Constrained Linguistic Typology Feature Prediction in SIGTYP 2020 Shared Task

Alexander Gutkin
Google, London, United Kingdom
agutkin@google.com

Richard Sproat
Google, Tokyo, Japan
rws@google.com

Abstract

This paper describes the NEMO submission to SIGTYP 2020 shared task (Bjerva et al., 2020) which deals with prediction of linguistic typological features for multiple languages using the data derived from World Atlas of Language Structures (WALS). We employ frequentist inference to represent correlations between typological features and use this representation to train simple multi-class estimators that predict individual features. We describe two submitted ridge regression-based configurations which ranked second and third overall in the constrained task. Our best configuration achieved the micro-averaged accuracy score of 0.66 on 149 test languages.

1 Introduction

The rapidly developing field of computational linguistic typology (Ramat, 2011) is becoming increasingly popular in natural language processing (NLP) research (Bender, 2016; Ponti et al., 2019), where typological corpora such as the World Atlas of Language Structures (WALS) (Dryer and Haspelmath, 2013) and AUTOTYP (Bickel et al., 2020) are seeing increased use (Naseem et al., 2012; Burdick et al., 2020). Despite their popularity, typological corpora are very sparse. According to Murawaki and Yamauchi (2018), less than 15% of the feature values are present for the 2,679 languages represented in WALS. These databases are human-curated and depend on grammatical descriptions for their development; sparsity is often due to linguistic sources lacking data on particular features for a given language. Developing methodologies for accurately predicting missing typological features on the basis of existing knowledge is therefore crucial for a wider adoption of typological resources in NLP tasks and beyond (Evans and Levinson, 2009).

This paper presents the work done by the "NEMO Team" (Google London and Tokyo) on the *constrained subtask* for the SIGTYP 2020 Shared Task (Bjerva et al., 2020). We experimented with a variety of machine learning models using only the features provided in the training, development and test sets. Our features included genetic features (genus and family), areal features (clusters of languages within a radius of the target language), and derived implicational universals. Originally introduced by Greenberg (1963) and demonstrated to capture the syntactic typology well (Dryer, 1992, 2009; Dunn et al., 2011), similarly to others (Daumé III and Campbell, 2007) we use the framework of universal implications to capture correlations between other types of typological features as well. We describe how these features were derived in detail in Section 3.

As we report below in Section 4, the performance of machine learning algorithms varied across different feature predictions, with some algorithms working better for some features, and less well for others. On balance however we found that ridge regression (Hoerl and Kennard, 1970), also known as Tikhonov regularization (Franklin, 1974), was the most useful approach.

2 Related Work

Here we review the approaches corresponding to the constrained sub-task of the shared task, where no external data, such as unlabeled texts, is allowed.

A popular approach to modeling the typological diversity of the world's languages is based on Bayesian probabilistic inference. Despite recently drawing some criticism on linguistic grounds by Ono (2020), this approach possesses impressive explanatory power. In what possibly represents the earliest model-based typological feature imputer,

Proceedings of the Second Workshop on Computational Research in Linguistic Typology, pages 17–28
Online, November 19, 2020.

Daumé III and Campbell (2007) introduced the probabilistic Bayesian model for uncovering universal implications in WALS data by associating random variables with individual WALS features and discovering the inter-feature correlations from statistical dependence between random variables. The modeling power of the Bayesian approach was further demonstrated by Daumé III (2009) in a non-parametric hierarchical Bayesian model combining linguistic areas and phylogeny.

Murawaki (2015) proposed a deep learning approach to phylogenetic inference by mapping the language vectors to a latent space using an auto-encoder trained using typologically-inspired objective on WALS data with missing values imputed using a regularized iterative variant of Multiple Correspondence Analysis (MCA) (Josse and Husson, 2012; Josse et al., 2012). In later work, Murawaki (2017, 2019) and Murawaki and Yamauchi (2018) abandoned an earlier model in favor of a Bayesian autologistic approach and demonstrated the superiority of Bayesian predictor over MCA. In this approach, the languages are represented as random variables that are explained in terms of other languages related to each other through phylogenetic and spatial neighborhood graphs. Bjerva et al. (2019) introduce a generative model inspired by the Chomskyan principles-and-parameters framework, drawing on the correlations between typological features of languages to tackle the novel task of typological collaborative filtering, a concept borrowed from the area of recommender systems.

While most state-of-the-art missing feature imputation methods are model-based, recently Buis and Hulden (2019) employed the iterative technique based on singular value decomposition (SVD) from the well-studied area of low-rank matrix completion and reported the performance on par with the prior art. Although lacking explanatory power, similarly to MCA, such techniques are attractive due to their simplicity and computational efficiency. Takamura et al. (2016) took a standard machine learning approach by training multinomial logistic regression classifiers for individual WALS features based on other features present in the database under various experimental conditions, hypothesizing that the classifier would capture feature correlations implicit in the data.

The frequentist approach we take is similar in some respects to work of Takamura et al. (2016) in that we also train vector space classifiers, but there are a few notable differences, we: (i) use typologically-motivated "probabilistic" frequency-based input space by explicitly representing areal and phylogenetic associations and implicational universals, and (ii) explore a wider range of classification approaches.

Although for this task there is a special interest in the geographic aspect of the modeling, for our final submission we limited ourselves to the rather orthodox approach of representing language associations through fixed neighborhoods, in order not to over-complicate our method (described in the next section) that can be difficult to reconcile with the more sophisticated models, such as the very promising model of language evolution from Kauhanen et al. (2019) and the findings emerging from the fields of dialectology and dialectometry (Szmrecsanyi, 2011; Wieling and Nerbonne, 2015; Nerbonne et al., 2020).

3 Method

Here we outline the details of our approach used to generate the final submission. The open-source implementation of our training and evaluation pipeline has been released in public domain.[1]

3.1 Precomputation of Features

Typological features were preprocessed to find likely associations between genetic and areal properties of the language. For each typological feature f and value v from a set of its values V_f we computed the following probability estimates:

$$p_{\text{genus}}(v|f) = \frac{\text{count}_{\text{genus}}(v)}{\text{count}_{\text{genus}}(f)} \tag{1}$$

$$p_{\text{family}}(v|f) = \frac{\text{count}_{\text{family}}(v)}{\text{count}_{\text{family}}(f)} \tag{2}$$

$$p_{\text{area}}(v|f) = \frac{\text{count}_{\text{area}}(v)}{\text{count}_{\text{area}}(f)}\ , \tag{3}$$

where $\text{count}(f) = \sum_{v_i \in V_f} \text{count}(v_i)$. Here, "family" and "genus" in equations 1 and 2 were as given in the data, and "area" in equation 3 comprised all languages within a 2,500 kilometer radius around the target language's latitude and longitude computed using the Haversine formula (Robusto, 1957).[2]

[1]Available at `https://github.com/google-research/google-research/tree/master/constrained_language_typology`.

[2]A reviewer noted that the hard limit of 2,500 kilometers seemed arbitrary and wondered why we do not weight "neigh-

Type	Example
Family	`Niger-Congo|Green_and_Blue|3 Black/green/blue|0.667|9`
Genus	`Bantoid|Green_and_Blue|3 Black/green/blue|1.000|2`
Area	`8.0,4.33333|Green_and_Blue|3 Black/green/blue|0.692|13`
Implicational	`Red_and_Yellow|2 Red/yellow|Green_and_Blue|3 Black/green/blue|0.583|12|0.148|54`

Table 1: Examples of precomputed most likely associations for color features.

In addition we computed a set of *implicational universals* (Greenberg, 1963). For each feature value v_j, for feature f_j, we compute the probability of of v_j given f_j, and each f_i, v_i pair from the set of known feature-value pairs in the data

$$p(v_j|f_j, f_i, v_i) = \frac{\text{count}(v_j)}{\text{count}(f_j, f_i, v_i)}. \quad (4)$$

For each of the genetic (family and genus), areal (neighborhood) and universal implication types of associations we kept a separate table, where, for all the known features f we stored

- the feature f,
- the total number of samples in the data of the given type with f, denoted $c(f)$,
- the value v with the highest estimated probability per the above equations, denoted v^{maj},
- the prior p^{maj} corresponding to v^{maj}.

Examples of the most likely associations computed above are shown in the first three rows of Table 1. For the Niger-Congo language family, the most likely value for the feature Green_and_Blue (observed 9 times) is 3 Black/green/blue, with the corresponding prior 0.667. For the Bantoid language genus, the feature Green_and_Blue was observed twice, both times with the same value 3 Black/green/blue. The areal example corresponds to the neighborhood of Yoruba,

boring languages according to closeness and use weighted clustering instead." We agree that in principle more sophisticated approaches would be nice, but one should bear in mind that the geographic centroids for languages provided in the data are at best crude, and so doing anything more sophisticated seemed to us to be crude. Also, to do this properly, distance is really not sufficient: one would also need to account for the presence of possible barriers to contact, including impassable mountain ranges, seas, and hostile neighbors, elements that would be hard to model.

Partition	Genus	Family	Area	Implicational
TRAIN	11,369	21,592	213,441	144,719
TRAIN+DEV	12,352	23,098	240,840	147,430
TRAIN+DEV+TEST	12,904	24,130	241,438	148,923

Table 2: Precomputed typological feature associations.

$(\phi, \lambda)=(8.0, 4.3)$ (where ϕ denotes latitude), for which 13 Green_and_Blue features were observed, with the most likely value corresponding to 3 Black/green/blue with prior 0.692.

In addition for the implicational features, we stored the prior probability of v_i given the conditional feature f_i from equation 4, and the total count for f_i. As an example of a weak implicational preference consider the example given in the fourth row of Table 1, which means that if a language has 2 Red/yellow for the feature Red_and_Yellow, then there is a slight preference (p=0.583, estimated on the basis of 12 examples) for having 3 Black/green/blue as the value for Green_and_Blue. In other words, 2 Red/yellow ⊃ 3 Black/green/blue. There were 54 cases of Green_and_Blue in the training data, for which the estimated a priori probability for 3 Black/green/blue is 0.148.

Table 2 shows the overall sizes of the association tables for the genetic, areal and implicational types described above for the different partitions of the shared task data.

3.2 Sparse Language Vectors

For each typological feature we train a separate feature estimator, resulting in 185 estimators overall. When training an individual estimator, we represent each language in the training and development set as a sparse feature vector. Likewise, the languages whose features need to be predicted at test time are also represented similarly.

The makeup of individual language vector for a given typological feature f and a language l is shown in Table 3. The vector consists of dense and sparse subvectors; the components shown in the first four rows of the table are mostly dense. The first subvector consists of language's latitude ϕ and longitude λ coordinate, represented as two numeric features exactly the same as given in the shared task data. There is no particular rationale for this choice other than we previously found that for a different task (speech synthesis) choosing alternative representations for the language location (e.g., distances to all other languages in the train-

Subvector	Size	Components		Type
Location	2	Latitude	$\phi(l)$	Numeric
		Longitude	$\lambda(l)$	Numeric
Genus	3	Value	$v^{\text{maj}}_{\text{genus}}(f)$	Categorical
		Prior	$p^{\text{maj}}_{\text{genus}}(f)$	Numeric
		Count	$c_{\text{genus}}(f)$	Numeric
Family	3	Value	$v^{\text{maj}}_{\text{family}}(f)$	Categorical
		Prior	$p^{\text{maj}}_{\text{family}}(f)$	Numeric
		Count	$c_{\text{family}}(f)$	Numeric
Area	3	Value	$v^{\text{maj}}_{\text{area}}(f)$	Categorical
		Prior	$p^{\text{maj}}_{\text{area}}(f)$	Numeric
		Count	$c_{\text{area}}(f)$	Numeric
...	...	...		...
Implicational$_i$	5	Value	$v^{\text{maj}}(f_i)$	Categorical
		Prob.	$p(v_i \| f, v, f_i)$	Numeric
		Count	$c(f, v, f_i)$	Numeric
		Prior	$p(v_i \| f_i)$	Numeric
		Count	$c(f_i)$	Numeric
...	...	...		...

Table 3: Language vector for typological feature f and language l.

ing set) in the input features did not significantly improve the results (Gutkin and Sproat, 2017).

The next three subvectors representing genus, family and area, are structured similarly using the three components used in association tables described previously: the majority value $v^{\text{maj}}(f)$ represented as a categorical feature, the prior corresponding to this value $p^{\text{maj}}(f)$ and the feature frequency $c(f)$, both represented as numeric features. For these three subvectors, the missing values are represented by the three-tuple $(v_\emptyset, 10^{-6}, 0)$, where $v_\emptyset$ denotes a global dummy typological feature value.[3]

The first four subvectors described above are followed by multiple subvectors representing individual universal implications, as shown in the fifth row of Table 3. Each implicational, describing the dependence of feature f_i on f, is represented as a five-tuple whose elements are stored in the associations table for implicational universals: The most likely value $v^{\text{maj}}(f_i)$ of f_i corresponding to the highest conditional probability $p(v_i|f, v, f_i)$ (interpreted as probability of f_i taking value v_i given that f is v), the total count $c(f_i, f, v)$ of f_i when f is v, the prior $p(v_i|f_i)$ and the total count $c(f_i)$ for f_i when f is v. The missing implicational is represented as a five-tuple $(v_\emptyset, 10^{-6}, 0, 10^{-6}, 0)$. As mentioned above, the implicational portion of the language vector is very sparse because, for a feature $f \in F$ the language vector belongs to, one needs to compute all its correlations to other features $f_i \in F$, where F is the set of all 182 known features. Since the typological database is very sparse, most of the observed correlations between f and f_i for a given language l are poorly instantiated.

[3]The choice of 10^{-6} for a missing value prior is arbitrary. Any small non-zero value valid for a log transform is suitable.

Set	Langs	Families	Genera	Features		
				Types	Values	
					Unique	Total
TRAIN	1,125	131	283	185	993	42,698
DEV	83	36	53	182	628	3,246
TEST	149	35	45	179	577	3,056
Total	1,357	145	311	185	1,034	49,000

Table 4: The three partitions of SIGTYP data.

The categorical features in the language vector are represented using a one-hot encoding and the numeric features are scaled to zero mean and unit variance. For probability components, prior to numeric feature scaling, the probability features are transformed into log domain.

The overall representation results in the language vectors with a rather high dimensionality. For example, the language vectors for the `Order_of_Subject,_Object_and_Verb` feature have the dimension of 4111. As we shall see below from the shared task details, this representation may already be too specific given the training set which only contains 1,125 data points. This observation also explains our choice of representing features and implicationals with the attributes associated with their most likely majority values rather than all the values for that feature observed in the data, as suggested by a reviewer — doing so will dramatically increase the dimension of input feature space even further and render out approach completely intractable.

4 Experiments and Discussion

In what follows, we provide a brief overview of the datasets, introduce the baseline systems we evaluated against during the development of our method, provide the evaluation results of miscellaneous machine learning algorithms on the development set that guided our final model selection, describe the two configurations submitted to the constrained subtask and, finally, mention the approaches that did not work well in our settings.

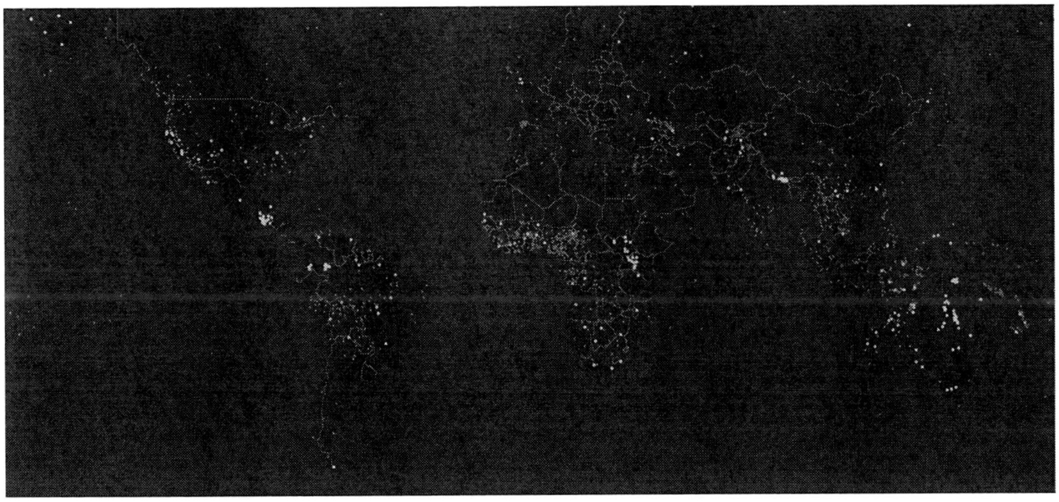

Figure 1: Languages in the SIGTYP training (blue), development (green) and test (yellow) sets.

4.1 Data Overview

Some of the properties of the data used in our experiments[4] are shown in Table 4, where we summarize the counts for three partitions of the data: the training and development sets, and the *blind* test set. For each of the sets, the total number of languages is shown along with the number of unique language families and genera. The count of typological feature types is displayed along with the number of unique feature values and the total number of observed values. As can be seen from the table, the size of the data is very small, which precludes us from using state-of-the-art deep learning methods, especially given our approach to representing each language as a point in high-dimensional space.

The 1,357 longitude and latitude language coordinates provided in the data are displayed in Figure 1 (best viewed in color) using the Mercator projection. The languages in the training set are shown in blue, the development set languages in green and the test set languages in yellow.

4.2 Baselines

For our baselines five simple prediction algorithms based on deterministic search were implemented. Initially we evaluated these systems on the development (DEV) set and later on the test set, after the golden truth data was released by the organizers.

[4]The SIGTYP data is available from https://github.com/sigtyp/ST2020/tree/master/data.

The *global* majority class predictor (denoted $\textsc{b}_1$) accumulates the frequencies of all the typological feature values in the training data and predicts the most frequent value for the feature in question irrespective of its phylogenetic or areal attributes. The *clade* majority class predictor (denoted $\textsc{b}_2$) extends the previous predictor by also taking into account language genera and families, producing predictions of the form

$$\hat{v}_{\textsc{b}_2}(f) = \begin{cases} v^{\text{maj}}(f) & \text{if } c_{\text{genus}}(f) = 0 \text{ and} \\ & \quad c_{\text{family}}(f) = 0\ , \\ v^{\text{maj}}_{\text{family}}(f) & \text{if } c_{\text{genus}}(f) = 0\,, \\ v^{\text{maj}}_{\text{genus}}(f) & \text{if } c_{\text{genus}}(f) > 0\,. \end{cases}$$

Predictor $\textsc{b}_3$ only relies on the distances between languages' geographic coordinates defined in the data. For each typological feature in question, the predictor returns the value belonging to the closest language, according to the Haversine formula (Robusto, 1957), with a known value for that feature. The Haversine distance $d(l_i, l_j)$ is computed between each pair of languages l_i and l_j represented as points on an ideal sphere using their respective latitude and longitude coordinates (ϕ_i, λ_i) and (ϕ_j, λ_j).

A naïve approach for combining areal and phylogenetic knowledge is implemented by predictor $\textsc{b}_4$ which performs its search in two additional clusters of inter-language distances, grouped by genera and families: The algorithm first searches for

Sets		# Evals	Systems				
Train	Test		B_1	B_2	B_3	B_4	B_5
TRAIN	DEV	3,246	53.67	62.69	58.87	59.33	**63.56**
TRAIN+DEV	TEST	5,477	54.66	**63.87**	58.90	61.68	59.94

Table 5: Micro-averaged accuracies (%) for the five baseline systems.

the known feature within the geographically closest languages of the same genus, followed by a search within the closest languages from the same family, falling back to the closest languages from the global set.

The final baseline configuration B_5 uses an ensemble approach by combining areal and phylogenetic information by using majority voting. The areal estimate is provided by the majority estimate from the candidate's neighborhood (as described in Section 3.1) or, if that information is not available due to the nearest language being located beyond the neighborhood radius, by the known feature from the closest languages outside the neighborhood. The phylogenetic clade estimates are provided by the majority class values from genera and families (B_2), respectively. The final estimate is produced by the majority voting, where at least two predictions have to agree, otherwise the predictor falls back to global majority class estimates (B_1).

The micro-averaged accuracies for five of the baseline systems are shown in Table 5. We performed the evaluation by first obtaining the estimates from a set shown in the first column and then predicting *each* known feature value for the languages from a set shown in the second column (DEV or golden TEST) by pretending that this value is unknown. Best accuracies are highlighted in bold. As can be seen from the table, the best baseline configuration on the DEV set is the B_5 ensemble method, with the pure clade-based B_2 coming second. On the golden TEST set, B_2 is the winning configuration, while the second best configuration is B_4. It is interesting to note, that the methods that completely ignore phylogeny (B_1 and B_3) did not perform well in either evaluation.

As one reviewer notes, the apparent predominance of phylogeny in our results may seem surprising given that areal features are well-known to be important in many areas of the world — e.g. India (Emeneau, 1956). This is likely due at least in part to the fact that many of the language families in the sample are small families spoken in a relatively limited geographic area, or else are families

Algorithm	Acc.	Algorithm	Acc.
AdaBoost	41.56	LDA	47.84
Bagging Ensemble	49.04	Linear SVM	55.36
Decision Tree	44.27	Logistic Regression	58.78
DNN	55.55	QDA	34.32
Gaussian Naive Bayes	51.91	Random Forest	63.00
Gaussian Process	23.38	Ridge Regression	**75.88**

Table 6: Micro-averaged accuracies (%) of various algorithms on the development set.

like Pama-Nyungan, which are more or less isolated from unrelated neighbors. This would tend to confound the influence of phylogeny versus geography, since it is only when *part* of a language family is spoken in an area that is populated by speakers of unrelated families that one will see robust effects of geography.

4.3 Model Selection Using Development Set

We approach the feature prediction task by training 185 multi-class classifiers, one for each typological feature. Several standard machine learning algorithms were evaluated on the development set to establish the most optimal algorithm for the task. In particular, we trained decision trees (Breiman et al., 1984), Naive Bayes (Langley et al., 1992) with Gaussian mixtures, Gaussian processes (Rasmussen and Williams, 2006), classifiers based on linear and quadratic discriminant analysis (LDA and QDA, respectively) (Tharwat, 2016), support vector machines (SVM) with linear kernel (Suykens and Vandewalle, 1999), multinomial logistic regression (Böhning, 1992), ridge regression (Hoerl and Kennard, 1970) and simple feed-forward neural networks with a single layer of 200 units (DNN). In addition, three ensemble configurations were also evaluated: multi-class AdaBoost (with 100 estimators) (Zhu et al., 2009), random forests (with 200 estimators, minimum of three samples per leaf and information gain as splitting criterion) (Breiman, 2001) and bagging ensembles (Breiman, 1999). For all the algorithms we used the implementation provided by `scikit-learn` toolkit.[5] We mostly used default hyperparameters provided performing no special tuning.

The evaluation results for each of the classifiers are shown in Table 6. As can be seen from the table, there are only five algorithms out of twelve which are remotely comparable to our development set baselines summarized in Table 5: DNN, linear

[5] `https://scikit-learn.org/`

SVM, multinomial logistic regression, random forest and ridge regression. Out of those, the random forest ensemble method and the ridge regression are the only competitive models, with ridge regression estimation strongly outperforming all of our baselines on the development set achieving the micro-averaged accuracy of 75.88%. On the basis of this result we chose ridge regression algorithm for our experiments on the test set and the final submission.

It is worth noting, however, that it is not difficult to find cases where the ridge regression estimator does not perform as well as other methods. For example, for feature SVNegO_Order, the DNN (93% accuracy) and SVM (87% accuracy) both outperform ridge regression (80%). We hypothesized that a better alternative to fixing a certain method for all the features is to employ an ensemble of classifiers which are feature-specific. Although we include this approach in our implementation, so far we only tested it under scenario of performing an iterative stratified k-fold cross-validation (Witten et al., 2011) over the training, rather than development, set. The optimal feature-specific classifiers obtained by this method did not fare well on the development set, which is probably an indicator that development set was not an optimal reflection of the training data.

Aside from the ridge regression and random forest ensemble methods, the poor average performance of other classification algorithms on the development set is rather unexpected. We hypothesize that this may be due to several confounding factors. The first issue is that our approach of representing training data for each typological feature as sparse language vectors results in small amounts of high-dimensional training data that may not be enough to reliably train most of the classifiers in our particular setting. The second issue is the high feature sparsity which adversely affects multi-class classification for most of the algorithms. Consider the Order_of_Subject,_Object_and_Verb feature. The frequencies of its seven values (corresponding to class label counts) in the training data represented as an ordered set are $\{311, 226, 113, 51, 16, 6, 1\}$. Although we employ balanced class weighting for all the algorithms, using the label values to adjust the weights inversely proportional to class frequencies observed in the data, this may not be enough. Some unsatisfactory attempts to further remedy this are described below.

We further note that the relatively good performance of ridge regression and random forest classifiers on the development data without any hyper-parameter fine-tuning may possibly be explained by the relative robustness of both methods to sparseness and collinearity effects (which severely affect other types of parametric and non-parametric predictors in our experiment), as previously analyzed in detail by Tomaschek et al. (2018) and observed by others in a typological setting (Burdick et al., 2020) and elsewhere (Josifoski et al., 2019). We briefly reevaluate these assumptions on the released test set in Section 4.6.

4.4 Shared Task Submission

Our submission to shared task consists of two ridge regression classifier configurations denoted NEMO_system1 and NEMO_system2.[6] The difference between the two configurations is in how the training data is generated from the original shared task subsets. The training data for NEMO_system1 classifier consists of the language vectors generated from the original training (train.csv) and development (dev.csv) sets only. For NEMO_system2, the training data also includes the phylogenetic, areal and implicational relations computed from the *known* features in the blind test set (test_blinded.csv).

4.5 Approaches That Disappointed

In addition to the experiments described above, we also tried applying missing feature imputation algorithms to the data provided, as a preprocessing step prior to training the classifiers described above. Neither of the feature imputation algorithms that we tried produced satisfactory results that could improve upon our best baseline. One of the imputation approaches that we evaluated was Multiple Imputation with Denoising Autoencoders (MIDAS) by Lall and Robinson (2020). This approach is particularly attractive because it natively supports categorical features. However, due to reliance on a denoising autoencoder architecture (Vincent et al., 2010), the network requires large amounts of training data to be estimated reliably, which prevented us from getting adequate

[6] Submitted as NEMO_system1_assoc-train-dev_constrained and NEMO_system2_assoc-train-dev-test_constrained, respectively.

Family	# Languages Train	# Languages Test	Acc.
Mayan	6	17	0.73
Mahakiranti	4	13	0.72
Tucanoan	3	8	0.67
Nilotic	3	15	0.65
Madang	3	9	0.68
N. Pama-Nyungan	2	24	0.67

Table 7: Numbers of languages from each test family in the test and training data, along with our best system's per-family accuracy.

performance on the provided typological data.[7]

Similarly disappointing were the attempts to address the class imbalance problem during multi-class classifier training using class resampling techniques. Similar to the feature imputation above, resampling was applied as a preprocessing step prior to training the classifiers. In particular, neither the application of synthetic minority over-sampling technique (SMOTE) (Chawla et al., 2002) nor the adaptive synthetic sampling (He et al., 2008) produced any improvements over our best baseline.

We also extended our method to use country code information provided with the task data for each language. This was achieved by accumulating the per-country typological feature priors, similar to other areal and phylogenetic features, and representing the country codes as categorical features in classification, the process described in Section 3. Ridge regression estimator that included country code information achieved micro-averaged accuracy of 75.66% on the development set – a small deterioration of 0.3% compared to our best result. This may be due to multiple errors in the provided data, e.g., the country code for the Chepang language from Sino-Tibetan family spoken in Nepal (Caughley, 1982) is defined as `US` in the development set.

4.6 Discussion

We start with some observations about the rather apparent differences between the test data and the training and development data. In Table 7 we list the six language families evidenced in the test data, and the numbers of languages for each represented in the training and development data, versus the test data. As can be seen some of the language families are significantly more represented in the test data than they are in the data that was released

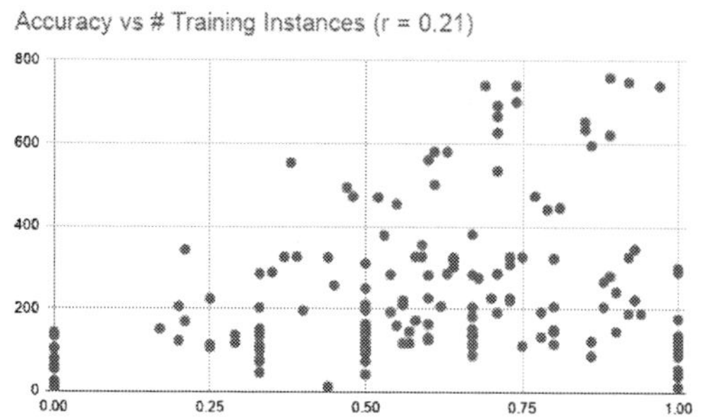

Figure 2: Feature accuracy versus number of instances of the feature in the training and development data (r=0.21).

earlier. This is particularly the case for Northern Pama-Nyungan, which comprised two languages in the training-development data, and twenty four languages in the test data. This skew can also be seen in Figure 1 where the yellow dots represent the test data. There are islands of yellow in Australia, Northern South Asia, Central East Africa and in Central America, surrounded by seas of green and blue.[8]

Turning now to our results, we discuss here the performance of our best model `NEMO_system2` (overall micro-averaged accuracy 0.66). First of all, we note that there is very little correlation between the number of exemplars of a feature in training and development, and our system's performance on that feature in the test set (correlation coefficient r=0.21): see Figure 2.[9]

Second, comparing our results against the best baseline provided by the task organizers — `frequency-baseline_constrained` (overall micro-averaged accuracy 0.51), we list in Tables 8 and 9 the five features for which our system had the largest win and loss, respectively in terms of absolute accuracy difference. Note that three of the five features for which we showed the largest gains relate to word order. While this may be due to the automatically derived implicational features used in our models — word-order-related features being probably among the most robust of the implicational universals — it is also true that these features are better instantiated in the data.

[7]The MIDAS imputer for linguistic typological data is released with the rest of our software.

[8]As one of the reviewers notes, it would be useful for future tasks if the organizers could provide a rationale for the data splits chosen.

[9]A reviewer asks if there is any correlation between accuracy and the number of value settings for each feature in the training and development set. This correlation is somewhat higher, and negative ($r = -0.34$), not surprising since we would expect to do worse if there are more possible values.

Feature	baseline	our best	# in test
Inclusive/Exclusive_Distinction_in_Verbal_Inflection	0.00	0.75	4
Rel_between_the_Order_of_Obj_and_Vb_and_the_Order_of_Adj_and_Noun	0.14	0.86	35
Order_of_Object_and_Verb	0.26	0.89	38
Order_of_Adposition_and_Noun_Phrase	0.26	0.89	27
Epistemic_Possibility	0.20	0.80	5

Table 8: Five features on which our best system most outperformed the best baseline, with accuracies for each, and counts for each in the test data.

Feature	baseline	our best	# in test
Person_Marking_on_Adpositions	0.50	0.20	10
Genitives,_Adjectives_and_Relative_Clauses	1.00	0.67	3
Noun_Phrase_Conjunction	0.67	0.33	3
Subtypes_of_Asymmetric_Standard_Negation	1.00	0.66	5
Obligatory_Possessive_Inflection	1.00	0.50	6

Table 9: Five features on which our best system most underperformed the best baseline, with accuracies for each, and counts for each in the test data.

Algorithm	Acc.	Algorithm	Acc.
AdaBoost	0.44	LDA	0.41
Bagging Ensemble	0.50	Linear SVM	0.56
Decision Tree	0.47	Logistic Regression	0.60
DNN	0.58	QDA	0.31
Gaussian Naive Bayes	0.46	Random Forest	0.62
Gaussian Process	0.23	Ridge Regression	**0.66**

Table 10: Micro-averaged accuracies of various algorithms on the test set.

One reviewer notes that it would be interesting to see the results of ablation studies for some of the high dimensional features discussed in Section 3.2. We agree, but leave this for future work.

Finally, recall from the discussion of development set-based model selection in Section 4.3 that ridge regression was the best performing model, followed by the non-parametric random forest predictor (see Table 6). Once the golden test data was released, we evaluated the same set of twelve classifiers on the test set with the results shown in Table 10. As can be seen from the table, the ranking of three best classifiers on the development set is preserved on the held-out test set as well: ridge regression is the best-performing classifier in our task, followed by random forest and, finally, multinomial logistic regression.

5 Conclusion

We have presented the NEMO submission to the 2020 SIGTYP shared task. Our system used genetic, geographical and automatically deduced implicational universals, and a range of classifiers of which ridge regression yielded the best overall performance. Our method achieved 0.66 overall accuracy on the task, compared to the best baseline provided by the organizers, which had an accuracy of 0.51. Our system tended to do better on test language families that were better represented in the training and development data, though interestingly the correlation between the number of instances of *features* in the training/development data and performance on that feature was not strong.

As discussed above, we include in the training package methods for ensembling classifiers so that one can find per-feature optimal classifiers, but we did not make use of this functionality for our submitted results. We do think, however, that further experimentation with this functionality would be useful.

Finally, as one of the reviewers notes, it would be interesting to ask what use work along the lines presented here could be to the field linguist/typologist who is interested in testing potential relationships between languages based on shared features. Many of the systems reported in Section 2 had this aim in mind. While we do not want to overstress the value of this sort of work compared to good linguistic intuition, we do think that knowing the Bayesian priors of associations, as we discussed in Section 3.1 could at least serve as a reminder that some feature settings may be shared simply because they are very common anyway.

Acknowledgments

The authors thank the anonymous reviewers for many helpful suggestions on an earlier version of this paper.

References

Emily M Bender. 2016. Linguistic typology in natural language processing. *Linguistic Typology*, 20(3):645–660.

Balthasar Bickel, Johanna Nichols, Taras Zakharko, Alena Witzlack-Makarevich, Kristine Hildebrandt, Michael Rießler, Lennart Bierkandt, Fernando Zúñiga, and John B. Lowe. 2020. The AUTOTYP database. *University of Zurich: Department of Comparative Language Science*. Version 0.1.1: `https://github.com/autotyp/autotyp-data`.

Johannes Bjerva, Yova Kementchedjhieva, Ryan Cotterell, and Isabelle Augenstein. 2019. A probabilistic generative model of linguistic typology. In *Proceedings of the 2019 Conference of the North American Chapter of the Association for Computational Linguistics: Human Language Technologies, Volume 1 (Long and Short Papers)*, pages 1529–1540, Minneapolis, Minnesota. Association for Computational Linguistics.

Johannes Bjerva, Elizabeth Salesky, Sabrina Mielke, Aditi Chaudhary, Giuseppe G. A. Celano, Edoardo M. Ponti, Ekaterina Vylomova, Ryan Cotterell, and Isabelle Augenstein. 2020. SIGTYP 2020 Shared Task: Prediction of Typological Features. In *Proceedings of the Second Workshop on Computational Research in Linguistic Typology*. Association for Computational Linguistics.

Dankmar Böhning. 1992. Multinomial logistic regression algorithm. *Annals of the institute of Statistical Mathematics*, 44(1):197–200.

Leo Breiman. 1999. Pasting small votes for classification in large databases and on-line. *Machine Learning*, 36(1-2):85–103.

Leo Breiman. 2001. Random forests. *Machine Learning*, 45(1):5–32.

Leo Breiman, Jerome Friedman, Charles J. Stone, and Richard A. Olshen. 1984. *Classification and Regression Trees*. Chapman & Hall/CRC Press.

Annebeth Buis and Mans Hulden. 2019. Typological feature prediction with matrix completion. In *Proceedings of TyP-NLP: The First Workshop on Typology for Polyglot NLP*, pages 13–15, Florence, Italy. Association for Computational Linguistics.

Laura Burdick, Jonathan K Kummerfeld, and Rada Mihalcea. 2020. Analyzing the surprising variability in word embedding stability across languages. *arXiv preprint arXiv:2004.14876*.

Ross Charles Caughley. 1982. *The syntax and morphology of the verb in Chepang*. Pacific Linguistics. Department of Linguistics, Research School of Pacific Studies, The Australian National University.

Nitesh V. Chawla, Kevin W. Bowyer, Lawrence O. Hall, and W. Philip Kegelmeyer. 2002. SMOTE: Synthetic minority over-sampling technique. *Journal of Artificial Intelligence Research*, 16:321–357.

Hal Daumé III. 2009. Non-parametric Bayesian areal linguistics. In *Proceedings of Human Language Technologies: The 2009 Annual Conference of the North American Chapter of the Association for Computational Linguistics*, pages 593–601, Boulder, Colorado. Association for Computational Linguistics.

Hal Daumé III and Lyle Campbell. 2007. A Bayesian model for discovering typological implications. In *Proceedings of the 45th Annual Meeting of the Association of Computational Linguistics*, pages 65–72, Prague, Czech Republic. Association for Computational Linguistics.

Matthew S Dryer. 1992. The Greenbergian word order correlations. *Language*, pages 81–138.

Matthew S Dryer. 2009. The Branching Direction Theory of word order correlations revisited. In Sergio Scalise, Elisabetta Magni, and Antonietta Bisetto, editors, *Universals of Language Today*, volume 76 of *Studies in Natural Language and Linguistic Theory*, pages 185–207. Springer.

Matthew S. Dryer and Martin Haspelmath. 2013. WALS online. *Leipzig: Max Planck Institute for Evolutionary Anthropology*. `http://wals.info/`.

Michael Dunn, Simon J Greenhill, Stephen C Levinson, and Russell D Gray. 2011. Evolved structure of language shows lineage-specific trends in word-order universals. *Nature*, 473(7345):79–82.

Murray Emeneau. 1956. India as a linguistic area. *Language*, 32(1):3–16.

Nicholas Evans and Stephen C. Levinson. 2009. The myth of language universals: Language diversity and its importance for cognitive science. *Behavioral and Brain Sciences*, 32(5):429–448.

Joel N Franklin. 1974. On Tikhonov's method for ill-posed problems. *Mathematics of Computation*, 28(128):889–907.

Joseph H. Greenberg. 1963. Some universals of grammar with particular reference to the order of meaningful elements. In Joseph H. Greenberg, editor, *Universals of Human Language*, pages 73–113. MIT Press, Cambridge, Mass.

Alexander Gutkin and Richard Sproat. 2017. Areal and phylogenetic features for multilingual speech synthesis. In *Proc. Interspeech 2017*, pages 2078–2082, Stockholm, Sweden. International Speech and Communication Association (ISCA).

Haibo He, Yang Bai, Edwardo A. Garcia, and Shutao Li. 2008. ADASYN: Adaptive synthetic sampling approach for imbalanced learning. In *Proc. of International Joint Conference on Neural Networks (IEEE World Congress on Computational Intelligence)*, pages 1322–1328. IEEE.

Arthur E Hoerl and Robert W Kennard. 1970. Ridge regression: Biased estimation for nonorthogonal problems. *Technometrics*, 12(1):55–67.

Martin Josifoski, Ivan S. Paskov, Hristo S. Paskov, Martin Jaggi, and Robert West. 2019. Crosslingual document embedding as reduced-rank ridge regression. In *Proceedings of the 12th ACM International Conference on Web Search and Data Mining (WSDM)*, pages 744–752, Melbourne, Australia.

Julie Josse, Marie Chavent, Benot Liquet, and François Husson. 2012. Handling missing values with regularized iterative multiple correspondence analysis. *Journal of Classification*, 29(1):91–116.

Julie Josse and François Husson. 2012. Handling missing values in exploratory multivariate data analysis methods. *Journal de la Société Française de Statistique*, 153(2):79–99.

Henri Kauhanen, Deepthi Gopal, Tobias Galla, and Ricardo Bermúdez-Otero. 2019. Geospatial distributions reflect rates of evolution of features of language. In *Proceedings of Workshop on Spatial Patterns of Language Evolution (SPLEV)*, Zurich, Switzerland.

Ranjit Lall and Thomas Robinson. 2020. Applying the MIDAS touch: How to handle missing values in large and complex data. *American Political Science Association Preprints*. Code available at: `https://github.com/ranjitlall/MIDAS`.

Pat Langley, Wayne Iba, Kevin Thompson, et al. 1992. An analysis of Bayesian classifiers. In *Proc. 10th Nat. Conf. on Artificial Intelligence*, volume 90, pages 223–228, USA. AAAI Press and MIT Press.

Yugo Murawaki. 2015. Continuous space representations of linguistic typology and their application to phylogenetic inference. In *Proceedings of the 2015 Conference of the North American Chapter of the Association for Computational Linguistics: Human Language Technologies*, pages 324–334, Denver, Colorado. Association for Computational Linguistics.

Yugo Murawaki. 2017. Diachrony-aware induction of binary latent representations from typological features. In *Proceedings of the Eighth International Joint Conference on Natural Language Processing (Volume 1: Long Papers)*, pages 451–461, Taipei, Taiwan. Asian Federation of Natural Language Processing.

Yugo Murawaki. 2019. Bayesian learning of latent representations of language structures. *Computational Linguistics*, 45(2):199–228.

Yugo Murawaki and Kenji Yamauchi. 2018. A statistical model for the joint inference of vertical stability and horizontal diffusibility of typological features. *Journal of Language Evolution*, 3(1):13–25.

Tahira Naseem, Regina Barzilay, and Amir Globerson. 2012. Selective sharing for multilingual dependency parsing. In *Proceedings of the 50th Annual Meeting of the Association for Computational Linguistics (Volume 1: Long Papers)*, pages 629–637, Jeju Island, Korea. Association for Computational Linguistics.

John Nerbonne, Jelena Prokić, and Martijn Wieling. 2020. Dialectology for computational linguists. In Marcos Zampieri and Preslav Nakov, editors, *Similar Languages, Varieties, and Dialects: A Computational Perspective*. Cambridge University Press. To appear.

Yohei Ono. 2020. How to handle "missing values" in linguistic typology: A pitfall in the statistical modelling approach. *Northern Language Studies*, 10:61–82.

Edoardo Maria Ponti, Helen O'Horan, Yevgeni Berzak, Ivan Vulić, Roi Reichart, Thierry Poibeau, Ekaterina Shutova, and Anna Korhonen. 2019. Modeling language variation and universals: A survey on typological linguistics for natural language processing. *Computational Linguistics*, 45(3):559–601.

Paolo Ramat. 2011. Linguistic typology. In Georg Bossong and Bernard Comrie, editors, *Empirical Approaches to Language Typology*, volume 1. Walter de Gruyter.

Carl Edward Rasmussen and Christopher K. I. Williams. 2006. *Gaussian Processes for Machine Learning*. MIT Press.

C. Carl Robusto. 1957. The Cosine-Haversine formula. *The American Mathematical Monthly*, 64(1):38–40.

Johan AK Suykens and Joos Vandewalle. 1999. Least squares support vector machine classifiers. *Neural Processing Letters*, 9(3):293–300.

Benedikt Szmrecsanyi. 2011. Corpus-based dialectometry: a methodological sketch. *Corpora*, 6(1):45–76.

Hiroya Takamura, Ryo Nagata, and Yoshifumi Kawasaki. 2016. Discriminative analysis of linguistic features for typological study. In *Proceedings of the Tenth International Conference on Language Resources and Evaluation (LREC'16)*, pages 69–76, Portorož, Slovenia. European Language Resources Association (ELRA).

Alaa Tharwat. 2016. Linear vs. quadratic discriminant analysis classifier: A tutorial. *International Journal of Applied Pattern Recognition*, 3(2):145–180.

Fabian Tomaschek, Peter Hendrix, and R. Harald Baayen. 2018. Strategies for addressing collinearity in multivariate linguistic data. *Journal of Phonetics*, 71:249–267.

Pascal Vincent, Hugo Larochelle, Isabelle Lajoie, Yoshua Bengio, Pierre-Antoine Manzagol, and Léon Bottou. 2010. Stacked denoising autoencoders: Learning useful representations in a deep network with a local denoising criterion. *Journal of Machine Learning Research*, 11(12).

Martijn Wieling and John Nerbonne. 2015. Advances in dialectometry. *Annual Review of Linguistics*, 1:243–264.

Ian H. Witten, Eibe Frank, and Mark A. Hall. 2011. *Data Mining: Practical Machine Learning Tools and Techniques*, 3rd edition. Morgen Kaufmann, San Francisco.

Ji Zhu, Hui Zou, Saharon Rosset, and Trevor Hastie. 2009. Multi-class AdaBoost. *Statistics and its Interface*, 2(3):349–360.

Predicting Typological Features in WALS using Language Embeddings and Conditional Probabilities: ÚFAL Submission to the SIGTYP 2020 Shared Task

Martin Vastl **Daniel Zeman** **Rudolf Rosa**
Charles University, Prague
Faculty of Mathematics and Physics
Institute of Formal and Applied Linguistics (ÚFAL)
martin.vastl2@gmail.com, {zeman|rosa}@ufal.mff.cuni.cz

Abstract

We present our submission to the SIGTYP 2020 Shared Task on the prediction of typological features. We submit a constrained system, predicting typological features only based on the WALS database. We investigate two approaches. The simpler of the two is a system based on estimating correlation of feature values within languages by computing conditional probabilities and mutual information. The second approach is to train a neural predictor operating on precomputed language embeddings based on WALS features. Our submitted system combines the two approaches based on their self-estimated confidence scores. We reach the accuracy of 70.7% on the test data and rank first in the shared task.

1 Introduction

The World Atlas of Language Structures (WALS) (Dryer and Haspelmath, 2013) is a database of over 2,000 languages, which lists structural properties ('features') of each language, gathered from reference grammars. The properties/features are phonological (such as the number of distinct consonants), grammatical (such as morphological devices or dominant word order) and lexical (such as the inventory of lexemes for colors). WALS can be browsed online[1] and the database is also available for download. It has been used in cross-lingual NLP to identify languages that are grammatically similar, and to cope with expected dissimilarities (O'Horan et al., 2016).

Unfortunately the WALS database is sparse as many feature values for many languages are missing. The goal of the present shared task is to predict the missing features with the help of the information that is known. Some typological properties are mutually dependent (Greenberg, 1963) and implications among the feature values can be found (Daumé III and Campbell, 2007).

We try to learn these implications from the WALS data using a combination of two machine learning approaches. After summarizing the task setup in Section 2, we describe our systems in Section 3, including models which we tested but did not use in the final submission. We thoroughly evaluate the systems in Section 4.

2 Task and Data

The SIGTYP 2020 shared task (Bjerva et al., 2020) splits the WALS data into training, development and test portion. In the blind test data, some feature values are masked and the participating system is supposed to predict them based on the remaining features that are left visible.

The task specification envisions a constrained and an unconstrained track, where the constrained systems can use only the provided WALS data, while an unconstrained system can use additional external resources, such as texts or pre-trained word vectors. We stay within the constrained track as for most languages we do not have any other data anyway.

The training data consists of 1,125 languages, the development data has 83 and the test data has 149 languages. Each language has 7 *general properties*, which are always filled in: the WALS language code, language name, genus, family, latitude, longitude and country codes (more than one country can be listed for a language). Then there are up to 185 *linguistic properties*. No language has all of them and no linguistic property has a known value for all languages. Within the training data, the best described language is English with 159 linguistic properties; the least described languages have just four linguistic properties each, and the median is 28. The most covered linguistic property is 83A

[1] https://wals.info/

Proceedings of the Second Workshop on Computational Research in Linguistic Typology, pages 29–35
Online, November 19, 2020.

Order of Object and Verb, filled in for 785 languages; the median is 168 languages, and the two least covered properties appear with 8 languages each. We refer to all language properties (general and linguistic) as *features*.

To be able to use the development data for evaluation, we randomly masked about one half of the linguistic properties (equivalent to about 42% of all features) and let the system predict them. On average, a language had 26.9 non-empty features and 19.2 features to predict. Minimum knowledge was 8 non-empty features (i.e., the 7 general properties plus one linguistic property), with 3 features to predict. Note that the organizers did not reveal in advance what would be the proportion of known and unknown features in the blind test data; in the end it turned out to be very similar to the proportion we used in our development data.

3 Systems

We tried several approaches to the problem, two of which yielded promising results. We refer to them as the Probabilistic System (Section 3.1) and the Neural System (Section 3.2). Our final setup is a combination of the two (Section 3.3); the output of this setup was submitted to the shared task evaluation. We also briefly mention other setups that we considered and abandoned because they did not fare well in preliminary evaluation (Section 3.4).

3.1 The Probabilistic System

Our simplest system works directly with the assumption that there are correlations between individual language properties. This assumption is widely accepted in typology, instantiated in particular in the Greenberg universals (Greenberg, 1963). For example, universal number 17 says that "with overwhelmingly more than chance frequency, languages with dominant order VSO have the adjective after the noun." Carried over to WALS, the universal implies that if feature 81A *Order of Subject, Object and Verb* has value *3 VSO*, then feature 87A *Order of Adjective and Noun* should have the value *2 Noun-Adjective*. If we know the universal and we see that the dominant word order in a language is VSO while the value of 87A is unknown, we can guess its value with high confidence. However, we do not let our model look at the list of Greenberg universals. Instead, we try to learn similar implications directly from the WALS training data. Specifically for the universal 17, the training data confirms the tendency claimed by Greenberg, although it definitely does not guarantee 100% prediction accuracy: out of 54 training languages for which both features are known and their dominant order is VSO, 28 languages (52%) have adjectives after nouns, 19 languages (35%) have adjectives before nouns, and 7 languages (13%) have no dominant adjective-noun order.

3.1.1 Model

Formally speaking, we have language L and features s and t. The value of feature s for language L is known: $s(L) = x$. The value of feature t is unknown for this language: $t(L) = ?$. We know the value range of t and we can estimate the conditional probability of each value based on training languages that have known values of both s and t: $P(t = y|s = x)$.

For each unknown feature t_j of a test language L we look at all features s_i whose values are known for L. Different source features s_i will provide different predictions of t_j, so we compare their probabilities. However, some probabilities are less reliable than others because they are based on fewer observations. To counterbalance that, we score each prediction by the multiple of its probability and the logarithm of the observation count c. Correlations based on a single observation are thus ignored completely.

$$\begin{aligned} score_1(s_i = x, t_j = y) \\ = P(t_j = y|s_i = x) \\ \times \log c(s_i = x, t_j = y) \end{aligned} \tag{1}$$

Another danger lies in features that appear frequently but contribute little information. For example, feature 143G *Minor morphological means of signaling negation* is with 750 occurrences almost as frequent as 81A, but its values are very unbalanced: for 99% languages the value is *4 None*. Co-occurrences of this value with 87A may seem to provide a strong signal that a given language prefers adjectives after nouns, but in reality they only reflect the general observation that there are more languages in WALS with post-nominal adjectives than the opposite. Therefore we compute the mutual information I of the probability distributions of each pair of features, and we add it as a third scoring factor:

$$
\begin{aligned}
score_2(s_i = x, t_j = y) \\
&= P(t_j = y | s_i = x) \\
&\times \log c(s_i = x, t_j = y) \\
&\times I(s_i, t_j)
\end{aligned} \quad (2)
$$

where

$$
I(s_i, t_j) = \sum_x \sum_y P(s_i = x, t_j = y) \times \log \frac{P(s_i = x, t_j = y)}{P(s_i = x)P(t_j = y)} \quad (3)
$$

For example, $I(143\text{G}, 87\text{A}) = 0.004$ while $I(81\text{A}, 87\text{A}) = 0.072$, meaning that the order of subject, object and verb is a much better indicator for the order of adjective and noun than the minor morphological means of negation.

Experiments with the development data have shown that $score_2$ (with mutual information) gives better results than $score_1$ (without mutual information), and both are better than the conditional probability alone. In all three settings we always take the source feature which provides the best-scored prediction, and ignore all other known features of the language. We have experimented with various voting schemes to combine signals from multiple source features but we were not able to obtain better results than with the single best prediction.

3.1.2 Feature Manipulation

Everything we know about the language can be used as a source feature. Besides numbered linguistic properties this also includes the language family, genus, geographical coordinates and country codes. We only do not trust the country code 'US' (United States) as we observed that it occurs mistakenly with many languages from various parts of the world. We treat these languages as if their country code was unknown.

The geographical coordinates also deserve special attention. They represent a point on the map where the language is displayed in WALS. Presumably the point is distinct from other languages in WALS and it lies near the center of the area where speakers of the language live. There is no indication of how large the area is; nevertheless, it is still possible that the points of small languages are close enough to indicate potential language contact.

Since the values of latitude and longitude are rarely shared among languages, we manually partitioned the globe to a number of unevenly-sized zones and replaced the exact coordinate with the zone. In total we have 5 latitudinal and 11 longitudinal zones. Then we find out, e.g., that out of the 50 languages in the longitudinal zone between 160° East and 140° West (covering many Pacific islands), 44 languages (88%) have adjectives after nouns.

Finally, we also created a new feature 'latlon', which combines the horizontal and vertical zone in one value. For instance, the Caucasian languages (but not only them) would fall in latlon = 35–60;35–70.

3.1.3 Development and Test Data

As we have previously noted, approximately one half of the features in our development data are visible, while the other half is masked; the same holds for the test data. The merit of the visible part of the development data is twofold. The obvious point is that known features s_i of language L serve as input for prediction of a masked feature t for language L. However, a co-occurrence of known features s_i and s_j in one language may also further improve our knowledge about feature correlations, which can be used for predictions in other languages. Therefore we merged the known part of the development data with the training data before creating the model and applying it to the masked features.

During the evaluation phase of the shared task, we further enriched this merged training data with the visible part of the blind test data.

3.2 The Neural System

3.2.1 Architecture

In the neural system we use an architecture similar to Paragraph vectors (Le and Mikolov, 2014). The paragraph id is replaced by language id, and the words by feature values. The overall architecture can be seen in Figure 1.

3.2.2 Preprocessing

As feature input, we use all available features except the language code and the country codes. We also cluster the geographical coordinates; but instead of manually drawn zones as used in the Probabilistic System, we cluster the points via k-Means and use the cluster id as a feature. The effect of number of clusters and other hyper-parameters is discussed in the next section.

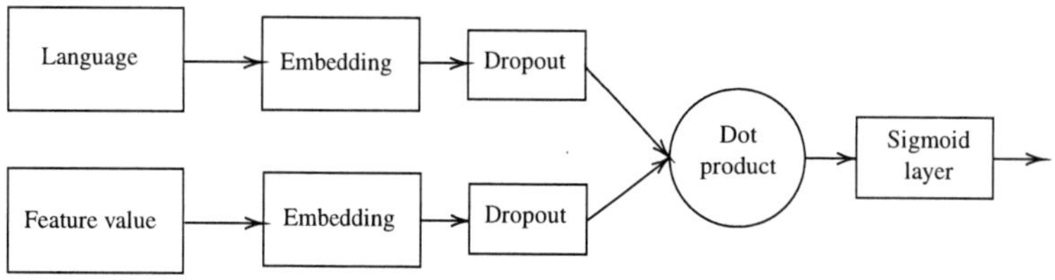

Figure 1: Neural system architecture

3.2.3 Training

The input to the neural network consists of a language id (which is a unique identifier for each language) and a feature value (e.g. if feature is 81A *Order of Subject, Object and Verb* and its value is *1 SOV*, then the feature value input to the neural network will be "81A: Order of Subject, Object and Verb: 1 SOV"). The goal of the neural network is a binary prediction whether the given feature value belongs to the given language. While training we select with 50% probability a feature value that belongs to the language, and with 50% probability a feature value that does not.

We use the Adam optimizer (Kingma and Ba, 2014) with learning rate of 0.001 for 200 epochs. We also run grid search on hyper-parameters to find the number of clusters (1, 10, 50, 100, 150, 300, 500, 1000), embedding size (128, 512, 1024) and dropout rate (0, 0.3, 0.5). We select the best model based on development data. We found out that the embedding size 512 with dropout rate 0.5 and 300 clusters yield the best accuracy of 73.9% on development data.

3.2.4 Prediction

The prediction of an unknown feature value for a given language is done via passing all possible values for the given feature to the network. We then select the feature value with the highest output probability.

3.2.5 Learned Embeddings

To investigate whether the learned language embeddings encode meaningful information, we run kNN (k nearest neighbors) with cosine distance on the embeddings to predict unknown features. With this approach we are able to achieve accuracy of 68.10% with majority vote on 33 nearest neighbors; this is much higher than a kNN with Hamming distance (see Section 3.4).

The visualization of the learned language embeddings projected to 2D via TSNE (van der Maaten and Hinton, 2008) can be seen in appendix in Figure 2. As we can see from the visualization, there are some clear clusters, however, further work would be needed to explain the clusters.

3.2.6 Development and Test Data

As in the Probabilistic system, we mix the visible part of the development data (and later test data) with the training data. This is needed in order to compute the language embeddings of the new languages.

3.3 The Combined System

We now describe the combination of the Probabilistic system and the Neural system which we submitted for evaluation within the shared task.

3.3.1 Analysis on Development Data

As will be shown in Table 1, both the Probabilistic system and the Neural system reach accuracies around 75% on the development data, with the Neural system being slightly better. However, a more detailed analysis showed that while the accuracies are similar, the errors the systems make are somewhat different: for 14% of the masked feature values in the development data, one of the systems predicts the correct value while the other system does not (in absolute numbers there are 225 such cases in the development data). An ensemble of the two systems could thus theoretically reach an accuracy of up to 82% if it were able to always select the correct prediction. This motivates our efforts in finding a way to combine the predictions of the two systems.

For this purpose, we utilize confidence scores produced by the two partial systems. For the Probabilistic system, its $score_2$ (Section 3.1.1) serves as the confidence score for each prediction; for the Neural system, we use the feature value probability produced by the last layer of the neural network.

We analyzed the confidence scores on the 225 predictions on development data where only one of the two systems predicted the correct feature value;

in 48% of cases it was the Probabilistic system, in 52% it was the Neural system.

Unfortunately, we found neither of the confidence scores to be a very good predictor of the correctness of the prediction, with the Neural system confidence score being somewhat more reliable. Specifically, low confidence scores tend to indicate a potentially incorrect prediction for each of the systems: on the least confident quarter of the predictions (25% of the analyzed predictions with lowest confidence score), the accuracy was only around 40% for each of the systems. High confidence scores are only indicative for the Neural system (61% accuracy on the most confident quarter), for the Probabilistic system they seem to behave rather randomly (accuracy on the most confident quarter is only 44%.)

3.3.2 Submitted Solution

As the Neural system seems to perform better than the Probabilistic system, our final solution is to return the prediction of the Neural system as the final output, unless the Neural system confidence is very low and the Probabilistic system confidence is not too low. Specifically, if the Neural system confidence is below a threshold T_N and the Probabilistic system confidence is above a threshold T_P, we return the prediction from the Probabilistic system, otherwise we return the prediction from the Neural system.

Based on the development data analysis, we found the optimal threshold values to be $T_N = 0.65$ and $T_P = 0.5$. On the development data, this leads to returning the output of the Probabilistic system instead of the Neural system in 6% of cases in which the predictions of the two systems differ, leading to an absolute gain of +1% in accuracy. On the test data, the output of the Probabilistic system was used in 10% of the differing cases.

3.4 Other Attempts

This section briefly describes some other approaches that we tried and abandoned because their accuracy was too low.

3.4.1 kNN

We used a simple kNN with Hamming distance to find the nearest neighbors of a language. The Hamming distance was calculated for each pair of languages as the number of features whose values in the two languages do not match. If one of the values for a given feature was unknown, we counted it as a mismatch. We then found k nearest neighbors of each language and filled the required values using majority vote among the neighbors. This setup was able to achieve accuracy of 62.28% on development set using 22 nearest neighbors. We have also tried different fallbacks such as most common value of a feature overall, most common value in a genus or most common value in a family in case of not finding any value among the neighbors. However, we found out that these fallbacks had little to none impact on the final accuracy of the model.

3.4.2 Feed-forward Neural Network

We have also tried the classical feed-forward network to predict the required features. As input, we randomly masked some of the non-empty feature values. We then embedded each feature value into the embedding space and concatenated these feature embeddings into a single vector. After the concatenation layer, we added a few feed-forward layers and the classification head for each feature. We have tried various architectures and percentages of masked values with no success. We were able to achieve an accuracy of 56.45% on the development set, which is worse than the accuracy of kNN.

4 Evaluation

The evaluation metric is a simple accuracy: the number of correctly predicted feature values divided by the number of masked features. Failure to predict a value of a masked feature would count as an incorrect prediction. Nevertheless, our systems always predict all masked features, even if there are few reliable clues and the system's confidence is low.

The accuracies of different setups are given in Table 1. The accuracy on the test data is the official number computed by the shared task organizers (Baseline and Combined) or by us using the official evaluation script (Probabilistic and Neural partial results); all the other results are computed on the development data. As a baseline, we evaluate a model where each feature receives its overall most probable value, regardless of language. Interestingly, the Probabilistic system outperforms the Neural system on the test data (contrary to what we observed on the development data) but the difference is again in the order of just a few wrong predictions.

Accuracies computed on individual languages are skewed because for some languages the system

System	Dev	Test
Baseline	53.45	51.39
Probabilistic	73.81	71.08
Neural	74.49	69.80
Combined	75.50	**70.75**
Feed-forward	56.45	
kNN-Hamming	62.28	
kNN-LangEmbed	68.10	

Table 1: Accuracy of various models on the development and test data.

had to predict only one feature. If we look at development languages where 10 or more features were masked, our Probabilistic system achieved 100% on four of them (Ukrainian, Uyghur, Wan and Venda); at the other end of the scale, accuracy on the South American language Uru is only 30%. The system never failed on 34 features; the most frequent of them is unsurprisingly (see Section 3.1) *Minor morphological means of signaling negation*, followed by *Order of Relative Clause and Noun* and *Postnominal relative clauses*. Note however that these observations do not necessarily indicate that a feature is easy or difficult to predict. The success depends heavily on how frequently the feature co-occurs with a suitable correlated feature in WALS, and whether our random masking selected the feature in presence or absence of the correlated feature.

5 Conclusion

We have described three systems (two individual systems and one combined system) that use the known features of a language to predict its remaining features. The first system is based on conditional probability of feature values, log frequency and mutual information. It achieves an accuracy of 73.81% on the development data. The second system uses a neural network to train language and feature embeddings, and to predict a feature value's probability based on the embeddings. It achieves slightly better results than the probabilistic model on the development data, but it is slightly worse on the test data. Finally, we use the scores produced by the two systems together with their predictions to decide which of the systems knows the correct answer in which situation. This combined system achieves 75.50% on the development data and 70.75% on the test data.

Our code is available at `https://github.com/ufal/ST2020`.

Acknowledgments

This work was supported by the LINDAT/CLARIAH-CZ project of the Ministry of Education, Youth and Sports of the Czech Republic (project LM2018101).

References

Johannes Bjerva, Elizabeth Salesky, Sabrina Mielke, Aditi Chaudhary, Giuseppe G. A. Celano, Edoardo M. Ponti, Ekaterina Vylomova, Ryan Cotterell, and Isabelle Augenstein. 2020. SIGTYP 2020 Shared Task: Prediction of Typological Features. In *Proceedings of the Second Workshop on Computational Research in Linguistic Typology*. Association for Computational Linguistics.

Hal Daumé III and Lyle Campbell. 2007. A Bayesian model for discovering typological implications. In *Proceedings of the 45th Annual Meeting of the Association for Computational Linguistics*, pages 65–72, Praha, Czechia. Association for Computational Linguistics.

Matthew S Dryer and Martin Haspelmath. 2013. The World Atlas of Language Structures online.

Joseph H. Greenberg. 1963. Some universals of grammar with particular reference to the order of meaningful elements. In Joseph H. Greenberg, editor, *Universals of Language*, pages 110–113. MIT Press, London.

Diederik P. Kingma and Jimmy Ba. 2014. Adam: A method for stochastic optimization. Cite arxiv:1412.6980Comment: Published as a conference paper at the 3rd International Conference for Learning Representations, San Diego, 2015.

Quoc V. Le and Tomas Mikolov. 2014. Distributed representations of sentences and documents. *CoRR*, abs/1405.4053.

Laurens van der Maaten and Geoffrey Hinton. 2008. Visualizing data using t-SNE. *Journal of Machine Learning Research*, 9:2579–2605.

Helen O'Horan, Yevgeni Berzak, Ivan Vulić, Roi Reichart, and Anna Korhonen. 2016. Survey on the use of typological information in natural language processing. In *Proceedings of COLING 2016, the 26th International Conference on Computational Linguistics: Technical Papers*, pages 1297–1308, Osaka, Japan. The COLING 2016 Organizing Committee.

A Appendix

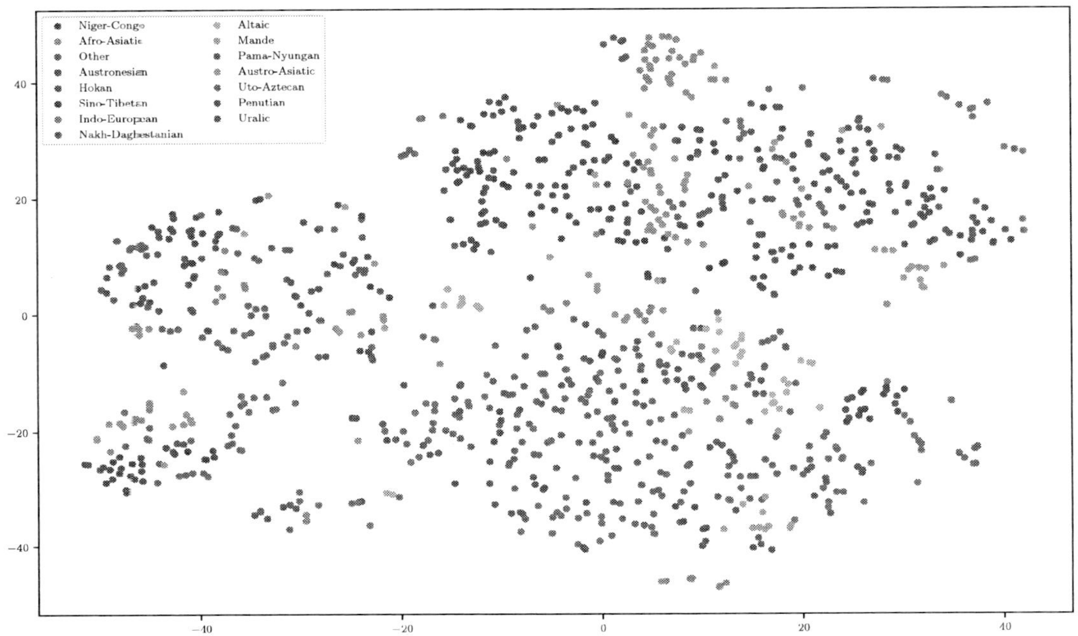

Figure 2: Visualisation of learned embeddings by family.

Imputing typological values via phylogenetic inference

Gerhard Jäger
Tübingen University / SfS, Wilhelmstr. 19, 72074 Tübingen, Germany
`gerhard.jaeger@uni-tuebingen.de`

Abstract

This paper describes a workflow to impute missing values in a typological database, a subset of the World Atlas of Language Structures (WALS). Using a world-wide phylogeny derived from lexical data, the model assumes a phylogenetic continuous time Markov chain governing the evolution of typological values. Data imputation is performed via a Maximum Likelihood estimation on the basis of this model. As back-off model for languages whose phylogenetic position is unknown, a k-nearest neighbor classification based on geographic distance is performed.

1 Introduction

Precise knowledge of the typological diversity of natural languages is essential for several scientific disciplines. It provides clues about cognitive biases in language learning and processing, intrinsic tendencies in language change, a window into deep time regarding prehistoric population spread and population contact, as well as scaffolds for setting up NLP infrastructure for understudied languages.

While a growing body of digital data collections has become available in this regard (e.g., Dryer and Haspelmath, 2013; Bickel et al., 2018), these resources are sparse and skewed both with respect to the languages and the features covered. Given that obtaining high-quality typological qualification for underdocumented languages is a highly demanding task, this situation is likely to persist. It is therefore worthwhile to leverage statistical and machine learning methods to impute missing typological feature values from existing resources. Precisely this is the topic of the *2020 shared task*[1] of the ACL *Special Interest Group on Typology* (SIGTYP). The organizers made three subset of the WALS data (Dryer and Haspelmath, 2013) available, see Table 1. The task is to impute the 2,410 missing values from the totality of known values.

2 General approach

The present approach is based on two simplifying assumptions:

- The value of a typological feature in a given language is stochastically independent from the values of other features, and
- typological feature values are transmitted only vertically, i.e. from ancestor language to descendant language.

Both assumptions are known to be wrong. The first one is falsified by the manifold findings regarding *implicative universals* (established in Greenberg, 1963 and amply confirmed in subsequent typological research). The second assumption ignores the impact of *language contact* on typological properties. Research in areal linguistics has established beyond doubt that typological properties can be transmitted horizontally though (see, e.g., Campbell, 2006 for an overview). It seems worthwhile, however, to test how well a model based on these idealizations fares with regard to typological predictions. This establishes a baseline to be improved upon in future research.

The approach pursued here assumes that the phylogeny, i.e. the family tree representing their genealogical interrelatedness, including branch lengths reflecting the time between divergence events, of the languages under consideration is known. I used the techniques described in (Jäger, 2018) to infer such a phylogeny from lexical data (see next section for details).

Following much work in computational phylogenetics (see, e.g., Felsenstein, 2004, and Dunn

[1] `https://sigtyp.github.io/st2020.html`, (Bjerva et al., 2020)

Proceedings of the Second Workshop on Computational Research in Linguistic Typology, pages 36–42
Online, November 19, 2020.

dataset	# languages	# features	# revealed values	# blinded values	release date
training	1,125	185	42,698	0	26 March 2020
development	83	182	3,246	0	26 March 2020
test	149	183	3,056	2,410	1 July 2020

Table 1: Subsets of WALS used in the Shared Task

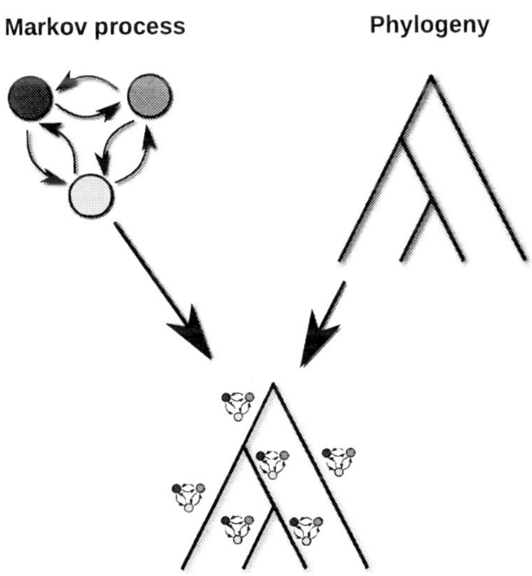

Figure 1: Phylogenetic CTMC

et al., 2011 for an application to linguistic typology), the model assumes that typological values evolve according to a *Continuous Time Markov Chain* process (CTMC). This means that a mutation, i.e., a change of the value of a typological feature, can occur at any time according to a probability density governed by a rate parameter. If a mutation occurs, another possible value of that feature is chosen according to a given probability distribution.

If a language splits into two daughter lineages, both daughter branches continue to evolve according to two independent copies of the mother language's CTMC. This is illustrated in Figure 1.

Let n be the number of values a given feature can assume. By way of a further simplification, I assume that the choice of a mutation target follows a uniform distribution. The probability of a language being in state b at the end of a time interval of length t if it was in state a at the beginning of the interval is given by (1) (known as the Jukes-Cantor model of molecular evolution, see for instance Felsenstein, 2004).

$$P(b|a;t,r) = \frac{1}{n}\begin{cases} 1+(n-1)e^{-tr} & \text{if } a=b \\ 1-e^{-tr} & \text{else} \end{cases} \quad (1)$$

The parameter r ($r \in \mathbb{R}^+$) is the *rate* of evolution, i.e., the expected number of mutations per unit of time.

Suppose the phylogeny, the parameters of the CTMC and the states at the tips of the phylogeny are observed. It is then possible to compute the posterior probability distribution of the state at the root of the tree via a postorder (bottom-up) recursion through the phylogeny.

The likelihood of an observed state at a tip is 1, and the likelihood of all other states is 0. The likelihood of state a at an internal node α, conditional on the observed states at all tips descending from α, is given by the following equation, where $\mathrm{dr}(\alpha)$ are the immediate daughter nodes of α.

$$\mathcal{L}_\alpha(a) = \prod_{\beta\in \mathrm{dr}(\alpha)} \sum_{b\in \mathrm{states}} P(a|b;t_{\alpha,\beta},r)\mathcal{L}_\beta(b),$$

Here $t_{\alpha,\beta}$ is the length of the branch from α to β.

Applying this equation recursively via postorder traversal through the phylogeny, we obtain the likelihood of the individual states at the root.

By assuming a uniform prior over states and applying Bayes' rule, the posterior probability of state a at the root of the phylogeny is

$$P(a|\mathrm{root}) = \frac{\mathcal{L}_{\mathrm{root}}(a)}{\sum_{b\in\mathrm{states}}\mathcal{L}_{\mathrm{root}}(b)}.$$

This algorithm is called *ancestral state reconstruction* (ASR). A detailed study of applications of ASR in linguistics for lexical evolution is given in (Jäger and List, 2018). An individual step of the recursion is graphically illustrated in Figure 2.

It is a convenient feature of the Jukes-Cantor model that it is *time reversible*. This means that the likelihood of a state at a node, given partial knowledge of the states at other nodes, remains

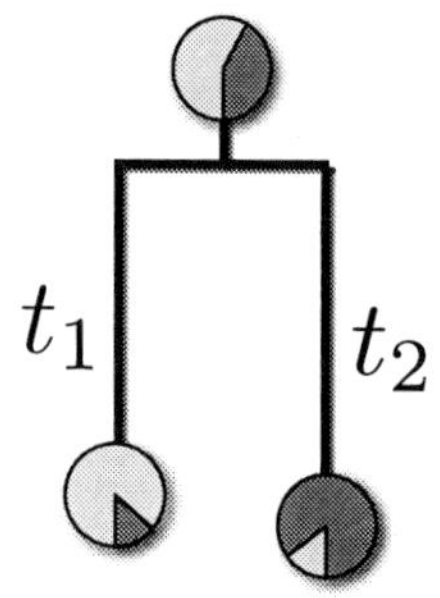

Figure 2: Elementary step of ASR

constant if the phylogeny is re-rooted and thereby the time arrow at some branches is reversed. Due to this property, it is possible to use ASR to impute unknown values at a tip of a tree. Suppose a phylogeny and the states of a feature at some, but not all, tips is known. To estimate the probability distribution over states at a particular tip α with missing value, the following steps are performed:

1. Prune the phylogeny by removing all tips with unknown value except α.
2. Reroot the tree so that α becomes the root.
3. Apply ASR.

This is graphically illustrated in Figure 3. The training set of the Shared Task contains the value of twelve Uralic languages for the feature *Order of Verb and Object*. The value for Udmurt (which is OV) is contained in the development set. Applying the described method (and using a known phylogeny and an estimated value for r; see next section), the posterior probability for OV in Udmurt, given the information in the training set, is ≈ 0.86. The maximum likelihood estimation of this feature value is therefore OV, which happens to be correct.

3 Data and methods

3.1 Phylogeny

In (Jäger, 2018) a method is described how to infer a world tree of languages from the 40-item Swadesh lists collected by the *Automated Similarity Judgment Project* (ASJP; Wichmann et al., 2020). The original paper used version 17 of ASJP. The results of applying precisely the same workflow to version 18 are made available at `https://osf.io/sdca4/` and were used here. More precisely, the phylogeny

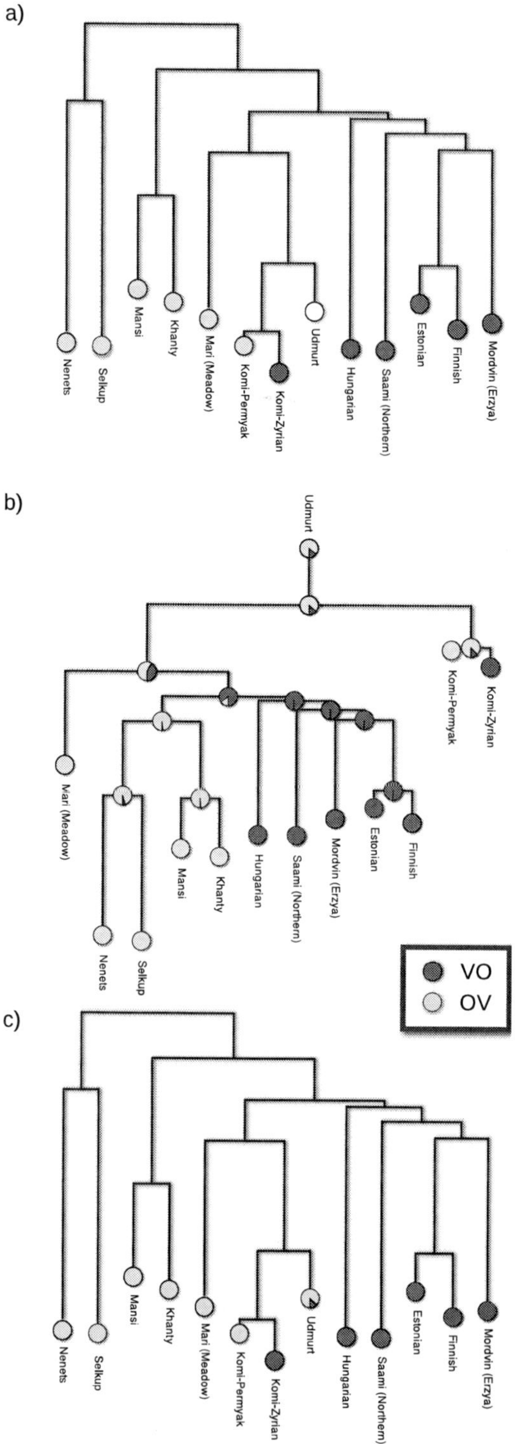

Figure 3: Value imputation via rerooting and ASR. a) Original phylogeny with missing value for Udmurt. b) Rerooting and recursive application of ASR. c) Resulting imputation.

RAxML_bestTree.world_sc_ccGlot was used, which is the result of using Maximum Likelihood phylogenetic inference over all characters and using the Glottolog classification (Hammarström et al., 2020) as constraint tree.

3.2 Matching WALS and ASJP

Among the 7,346 doculects for which the method described in the previous subsection provides cognate classification, only one doculect per glottocode was retained — generally the one with the least number of missing entries in ASJP. The metadata from WALS v.2020 were used to match glottocodes to WALS codes.

Among the 1,357 languages in the union of the three datasets from the Shared Task, 1,212 could be uniquely matched to an ASJP doculect with the same glottocode in this way.

For the 124 languages in the training set and the six languages in the development set for which no corresponding ASJP doculect could be identified in this way, I used the following procedure to define an ASJP proxy:

1. Use the closest geographic neighbor (according to great-circle distance, using the geographic coordinates supplied with the Shared Task data) within the same WALS genus among the 1,212 languages identified above.

2. If the language in question is a singleton within its genus, choose the closest geographic neighbor within its Glottolog family.

3. If the language is an isolate, choose the closest geographical neighbor.

The ASJP world tree was pruned to the 1,212 doculects which correspond to languages within the Shared Task data.

3.3 Phylogenetic value imputation

ASR, and therefore phylogenetic value imputation, depends on the rate parameter r. This value was estimated by maximizing the total marginal log-likelihood of all defined values within the training set under the CTMC model and the ASJP phylogeny. The log-likelihood as a function of r is shown in Figure 4. The Maximum-Likelihood estimation is $r \approx 5.13$.

Using this parameter estimate, the missing values from the test set for the 134 languages which

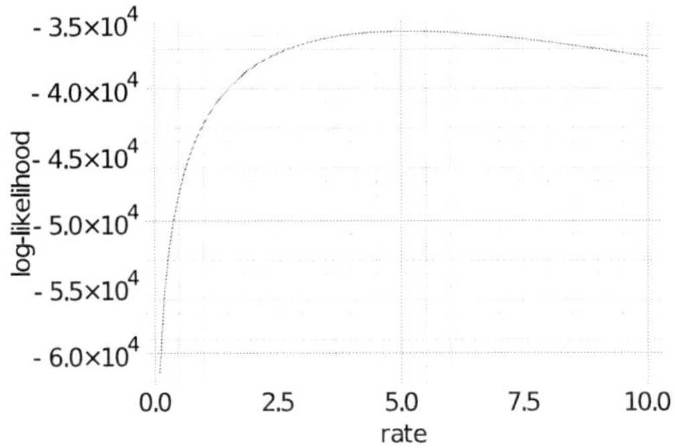

Figure 4: Log-likelihood of training set as a function of the mutation rate

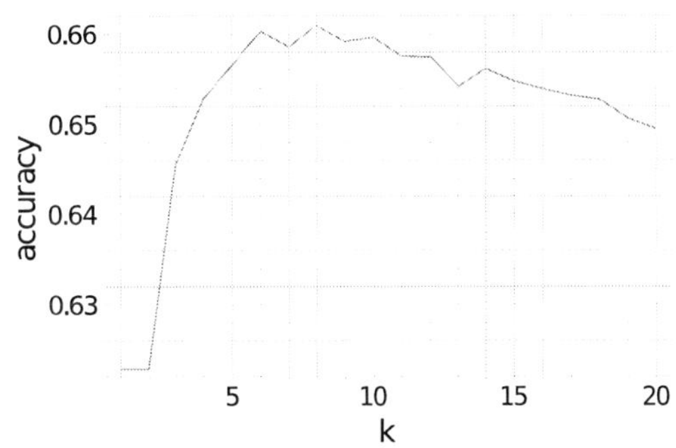

Figure 5: Average accuracy of geographic knn classification on the training set (20-fold cross-validation) as a function of k

directly correspond to an ASJP doculect were imputed. All known values from the training, development and test sets were used as input for the inference.

3.4 Geographical k-nearest neighbor back-off

15 languages in the test set do not correspond to an ASJP doculect with the same glottocode. For the missing values from these languages, phylogenetic value imputation was therefore not possible. As back-off for these languages model I chose k-nearest neighbor based on geographical distances.

The value of k was estimated using 20-fold cross-validation over all feature-value pairs of the training set (see Figure 5). The optimal cross-validation accuracy was achieved at $k = 8$. Using this value, the missing values for the 15 test languages missing an ASJP counterpart were predicted via geographical knn-classification from the union of the training and the validation set.

4 Error analysis

To assess which factors influence the performance of the phylogenetic imputation method, I conducted a 20-fold cross-validation on all language-feature pairs for which the language corresponds to a tip in the ASJP phylogeny. This provides a dataset of 44,598 language-feature pairs for which both a goldstandard value and an inferred value are available. Not surprisingly, the accuracy of the predictions depend on the following three factors:

- Entropy of the feature value. The more values a feature can take and the more evenly the possible values are distributed, the harder it is to predict the correct value.
- Size of the language family. The inferred phylogeny used here is fairly reliable within language families but less so across families. Therefore predictions based on phylogenetically close languages is the more reliable the more close relatives a language has.
- Coverage of the feature. The more languages have a known value within the training data, the easier it is to impute a missing value in the test data.

The effect of these predictors is visualized in Figure 6.

To test whether each of those three factors are relevant given the other two, I conducted a Bayesian mixed-effects logistic regression with accuracy of prediction as dependent variable, feature entropy, log-transformed size of language family and log-transformed feature coverage as fixed effects, and language family and feature as random effects. The analysis was carried out using the R-package `brms` (Bürkner, 2017), which is based on the the programmning lanuage *Stan* (Carpenter et al., 2017).

The results are shown in Table 2.

It demonstrates that feature entropy has a credible negative effect, and both family size and feature coverage have a credible positive effect on accuracy.

5 Results and discussion

According the evaluation script provided by the organizers of the Shared Task, this combination of phylogenetic and geographic knn value imputation achieved an overall accuracy of ≈ 0.68 — as compared to ≈ 0.51 both for the frequency baseline and the knn imputation baseline.

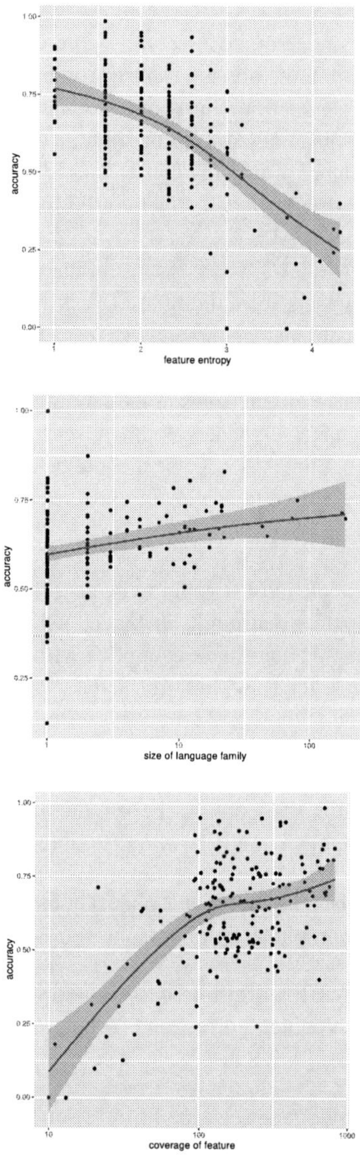

Figure 6: Impact of feature entropy, language family size and feature coverage on accuracy of phylogenetic imputation.

```
  Family: bernoulli
  Links: mu = logit
Formula: y ~ entropy + log10(featureFreq) + log10(famSize) + (1 | glotFam)
                 + (1 | feature)
   Data: dat (Number of observations: 44598)
Samples: 4 chains, each with iter = 2000; warmup = 1000; thin = 1;
         total post-warmup samples = 4000

Group-Level Effects:
~feature (Number of levels: 185)
              Estimate Est.Error l-95% CI u-95% CI Rhat Bulk_ESS Tail_ESS
sd(Intercept)     0.35      0.03     0.31     0.41 1.00     1456     2384

~glotFam (Number of levels: 164)
              Estimate Est.Error l-95% CI u-95% CI Rhat Bulk_ESS Tail_ESS
sd(Intercept)     0.31      0.03     0.26     0.36 1.00     1376     2310

Population-Level Effects:
                  Estimate Est.Error l-95% CI u-95% CI Rhat Bulk_ESS Tail_ESS
Intercept             0.68      0.24     0.21     1.16 1.00     1061     1849
entropy              -1.08      0.05    -1.17    -0.98 1.00     1408     2072
log10featureFreq      0.57      0.09     0.39     0.75 1.00     1029     1912
log10famSize          0.37      0.05     0.26     0.47 1.00     1056     1534

Samples were drawn using sampling(NUTS). For each parameter, Bulk_ESS
and Tail_ESS are effective sample size measures, and Rhat is the potential
scale reduction factor on split chains (at convergence, Rhat = 1).
```

Table 2: Mixed-effects logistic regression

As pointed out in the Introduction, this model makes several simplifying assumptions. The most serious one is arguably the presumed independence of typological features. The phylogenetics literature contains techniques for dealing with correlated discrete features (Dunn et al., 2011; Pagel and Meade, 2006). However, applying this approach on a large scale would lead to an explosion of parameters that cannot be estimated with the sparse data available in WALS or similar data sources. Therefore it seems more promising in the long run to attempt an embedding of discrete typological features into a continuous high-dimensional space and combine this with phylogenetic ASR for continuous characters (using, e.g., a Brownian motion model of evolution). Such an approach can be combined with multivariate techniques like PCA to detect correlations between features.

Furthermore, a principled study of the interplay between vertical/phylogenetic and horizontal transmission mechanisms is called for to make further progress in the task of typological value imputation.

6 Data and code

Data and code are freely available at `github.com/gerhardJaeger/emnlp2020`.

Acknowledgments

Many thanks to the organizers of the Shared Task, and to three anonymous reviewers for their feedback. This research was supported by the DFG-Centre for Advanced Studies in the Humanities *Words, Bones, Genes, Tools* (DFG-KFG 2237) and by the European Research Council (ERC) under the European Union's Horizon 2020 research and innovation programme (Grant agreement 834050).

References

Balthasar Bickel, Johanna Nichols, Taras Zakharko, Alena Witzlack-Makarevich, Kristine Hildebrandt, Michael Rießler, Lennart Bierkandt, Fernando Zúñiga, and John B. Lowe. 2018. The AUTOTYP database, release 0.1. `https://github.com/autotyp/autotyp-data`.

Johannes Bjerva, Elizabeth Salesky, Sabrina Mielke, Aditi Chaudhary, Giuseppe G. A. Celano, Edoardo M. Ponti, Ekaterina Vylomova, Ryan Cotterell, and Isabelle Augenstein. 2020. SIGTYP 2020 Shared Task: Prediction of Typological Features. In *Proceedings of the Second Workshop on Computational Research in Linguistic Typology*. Association for Computational Linguistics.

Paul-Christian Bürkner. 2017. Advanced Bayesian multilevel modeling with the R package brms. *The R Journal*, 10(1):395–411.

Lyle Campbell. 2006. Areal linguistics: A closer scrutiny. In Yaron Matras and April McMahon and- Nigel Vincent, editors, *Linguistic Areas*, pages 1–31. Springer.

Bob Carpenter, Andrew Gelman, Matthew D Hoffman, Daniel Lee, Ben Goodrich, Michael Betancourt, Marcus Brubaker, Jiqiang Guo, Peter Li, and Allen Riddell. 2017. Stan: A probabilistic programming language. *Journal of statistical software*, 76(1).

Matthew S. Dryer and Martin Haspelmath, editors. 2013. *The World Atlas of Language Structures Online*. Max Planck Institute for Evolutionary Anthropology. http://wals.info/.

Michael Dunn, Simon J. Greenhill, Stephen Levinson, and Russell D. Gray. 2011. Evolved structure of language shows lineage-specific trends in word-order universals. *Nature*, 473(7345):79–82.

Joseph Felsenstein. 2004. *Inferring Phylogenies*. Sinauer Inc. Publishers, Sunderland.

Joseph Greenberg. 1963. Some universals of grammar with special reference to the order of meaningful elements. In *Universals of Language*, pages 73–113. MIT Press, Cambridge, MA.

Harald Hammarström, Robert Forkel, Martin Haspelmath, and Sebastian Bank. 2020. *Glottolog 4.2.1*. Max Planck Institute for the Science of Human History, Jena.

Gerhard Jäger. 2018. Global-scale phylogenetic linguistic inference from lexical resources. *Scientific Data*, 5.

Gerhard Jäger and Johann-Mattis List. 2018. Using ancestral state reconstruction methods for onomasiological reconstruction in multilingual word lists. *Language Dynamics and Change*, 8(1):22–54.

Mark Pagel and Andrew Meade. 2006. Bayesian analysis of correlated evolution of discrete characters by reversible-jump Markov chain Monte Carlo. *The American Naturalist*, 167(6):808–825.

Søren Wichmann, Eric W. Holman, and Cecil H. Brown. 2020. The ASJP database (version 20). http://asjp.clld.org/.

NUIG: Multitasking Self-attention based approach to SigTyp 2020 Shared Task

Chinmay Choudhary
National University of Ireland, Galway
c.choudhary1@nuigalway.ie

Colm O'Riordan
National University of Ireland, Galway
colm.oriordan@nuigalway.ie

Abstract

The paper describes the *Multitasking Self-attention based approach* to constrained subtask within Sigtyp 2020 Shared task. Our model is simple neural network based architecture inspired by Transformers (Vaswani et al., 2017) model. The model uses Multitasking to compute values of all WALS features for a given input language simultaneously.

Results show that our approach performs at par with the baseline approaches, even though our proposed approach requires only phylogenetic and geographical attributes namely *Longitude*, *Latitude*, *Genus-index*, *Family-index* and *Country-index* and do not use any of the known WALS features of the respective input language, to compute its missing WALS features.

1 Introduction

In this paper we describe our *Multitasking Self-attention based approach* to Sigtyp 2020 Shared task (Constrained Sub-task) (Bjerva et al., 2020) which involves prediction of values of features from WALS Typology database for various low-resourced languages.

Linguistic typology is the classification of human languages according to their syntactic, phonological and semantic features. WALS (Haspelmath, 2009) is the most popular and comprehensive database which provides list of typological features and their possible values, as well as the respective feature-values for most of the world's languages.

However all the popular typological databases (Haspelmath, 2009; Collins and Kayne, 2009; Maddieson et al., 2013; Hartmann and Bradley Taylor, 2013; Bickel et al., 2017; Michaelis and Magnus Huber, 2013) (including WALS) suffer from a major shortcoming of limited coverage. In fact, values of many important typological features for most languages (specially less documented ones) are missing in these databases. This sparked a line of research on automatic acquisition of such missing typology knowledge (Malaviya et al., 2017; Coke et al., 2016; Daumé III, 2009; Daumé III and Campbell, 2009; Littell et al., 2017; Bjerva et al., 2019).

Our proposed model is a neural network architecture which takes in as input, the phylogenetic and geographical attributes of a language. The model subsequently predicts values of all its typology features simultaneously using Multitask learning setup (Ruder, 2017).

2 Model

Figure 1 depicts the architecture of our proposed model that computes values of all WALS typology features for a given language simultaneously. As evident in Figure 1, our proposed model architecture comprises of three components namely *Input Network Component*, *Self-attention Network Component* and *Multitasking Output Networks Component* described as section 2.1, 2.2 and 2.3 respectively.

2.1 Input Network Component

The input component is a simple two layered feed-forward neural network. The input of the network is a 5-dimensional vector x comprising of values of five key attributes of any language, namely *Longitude*, *Latitude*, *Genus-index*, *Family-index* and *Country-index* as these are the attributes provided by train and test datasets (for all languages within the datasets) for Sigtyp 2020 Shared Task. We computed Genus-index, Family-index and Country-index from *genus*, *family* and *countryCode* attributes provided within dataset using respective name-index dictionaries.

This two layered feed forward network computes output vector $o \in R^{T*d}$ where T is the total number of WALS typology features to be predicted by

Proceedings of the Second Workshop on Computational Research in Linguistic Typology, pages 43–50
Online, November 19, 2020.

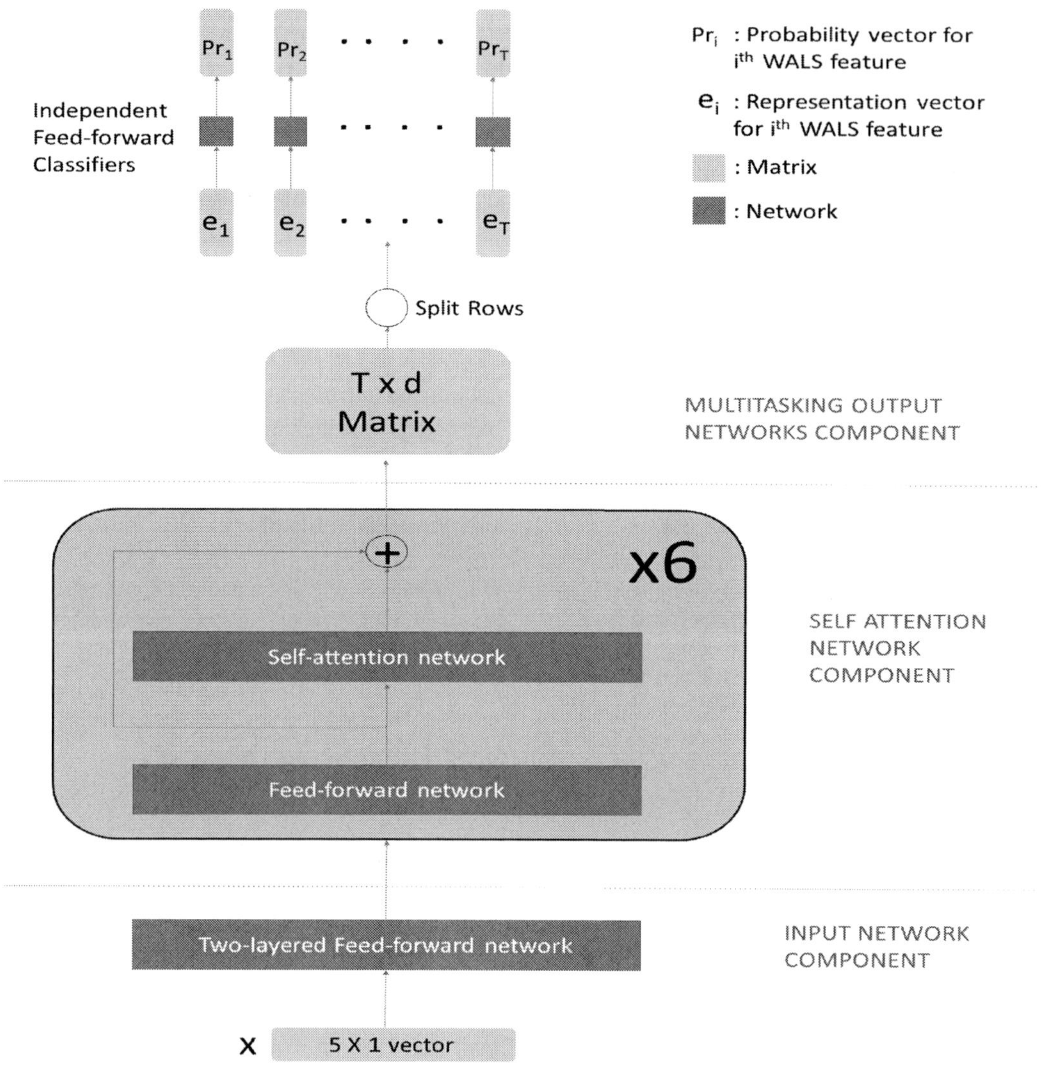

Figure 1: Architecture of proposed model

applying equations 1 and 2.

$$\hat{o} = tanh(A_1 * x + a_1) \quad (1)$$

$$o = tanh({A_2}^T * \hat{o} + a_2) \quad (2)$$

Here $A_1 \in R^{d*5}$, $A_2 \in R^{T*1}$ are weights and $a_1 \in R^d$ and $a_2 \in R^{T*d}$ are biases.

2.2 Self-attention Network Component

The architecture of this component is inspired by Transformers (Vaswani et al., 2017) model. The model architecture comprises a stack of $N = 6$ identical layers. Each layer has two sub-layers. The first is a multi-head self-attention mechanism, and the second is a simple fully connected feed-forward network. Hence input to layer i is always the output from layer $i-1$. Input to the first layer is the output of the previous Input Network Component.

For i^{th} layer within architecture, its *Feed-forward* and *self-attention* sub-layers are given by equations 3 and 4.

$$h_i = tanh(W_i * y_{i-1} + b_i) \quad (3)$$

$$k_i = attention(h_i, h_i) \quad (4)$$

Here $h_i \in R^d$ and $k_i \in R^d$ are outputs of *feed-forward* and *self-attention* layers respectively. We used same attention mechanism as used by (Vaswani et al., 2017). Final output of ith layer

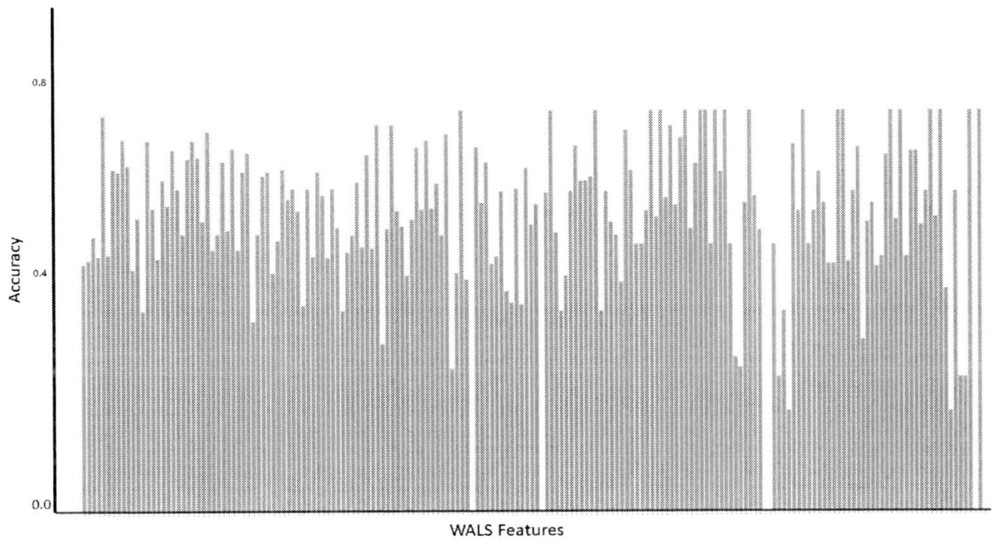

Figure 2: Plot depicting trend in accuracy values achieved on all WALS features

y_i is computed by adding h_i and k_i (equation 3).

$$y_i = h_i + k_i \quad (5)$$

Input to the first layer y_0 is the output from previous *Input Network Component*. Output of *Self-attention Network Component* is the output of final layer y_N.
It is been observed that there is a correlation between various WALS typology features. Thus, to predict the missing value of a particular typology feature for a specific languages, knowledge about other typology features for that languages would be useful. Such knowledge is ensured by the self-attention layers.

2.3 Multitasking Output Networks Component

Multitasking Output Networks Component comprises of T independent feed-forward neural-network classifiers. The component splits the output of previous Self-attention Network Component i.e $y_6 \in R^{T*d}$ into T d-dimensional vectors $e_1, e_2, \ldots. e_T$. each corresponds to one of the T typology features to be predicted.
Value of the jth typology feature is computed by applying equation 6.

$$Pr_j = Softmax(W_j * e_j + c_j) \quad (6)$$

Here $1 <= j <= T$, Pr_j provides probability of each of the possible values for j^{th} typology feature being the true-value. Dimensions of weights and biases are unique for each classifier as number of possible values for each of the typology features is unique.

Hyper-parameter	Value
d	548
drop_out probability	0.1
learning_rate	0.1
reduce lr on plateau	Yes
reduce factor	0.001
batch-size	20
steps-per-epoch	50
epochs	200
Number of features (T)	185

Table 1: Hyper-parameters

3 Training

The parameters of model described in section 2 are trained by optimizing the loss function given by equation 7.

$$Loss = \Sigma_{t=1}^{T} CE(Pr_t, OH_t) \quad (7)$$

Here OH_t is the one-hot encoding of true-value for t^{th} typology feature. CE is the Cross-entropy loss. Table 1 lists the hyper-parameters used during training. These are computed by minimizing the loss over Validation set.

Model	Accuracy
frequency-baseline_constrained	0.514
knn-imputation-baseline_constrained	0.508
NUIG_constrained	0.487

Table 2: Overall Accuracy of baseline and proposed models

4 Results

Table 2 compared the accuracy achieved by our proposed model with two baselines provided namely *frequency-baseline-constrained* and *knn-imputation-baseline-constrained.*

It is evident from table that our model performs at par with baselines, even though it utilizes only five attributes of the input language, namely *Longitude*, *Latitude*, *Genus-index*, *Family-index* and *Country-index* (model doesn't utilize any known WALS feature values, provided within test dataset for various languages).

Figure 2 is bar-plot that depicts the trend in accuracy achieved by our model on various WALS features. Precise accuracy score achieved by our model on all 185 WALS typology features is provided in Appendix.

5 Conclusion

In this paper we described our *Multitasking Self-attention based approach* to Sigtyp 2020 Shared task, Constrained Sub-task. Our model is simple neural network based approach which computes values of all WALS features for a given input language simultaneously in Multitasking settings. The architecture of our network is inspired by Transformers (Vaswani et al., 2017).

Results show that our approach performs at par with the baseline approaches, even though our approach uses only five linguistic and geographical attributes namely *Longitude*, *Latitude*, *Genus-index*, *Family-index* and *Country-index* and do not use any of the known WALS features of the respective input language, to compute its missing WALS features.

References

Balthasar Bickel, Johanna Nichols, Taras Zakharko, Alena Witzlack-Makarevich, Fernando Hildebrandt, Kristine, and John B Lowe. 2017. The autotyp typological databases. *Version 0.1. 0. Online:* `https://github.com/autotyp/autotyp-data/tree/0.1.0.`

Johannes Bjerva, Yova Kementchedjhieva, Ryan Cotterell, and Isabelle Augenstein. 2019. A probabilistic generative model of linguistic typology. *arXiv preprint arXiv:1903.10950.*

Johannes Bjerva, Elizabeth Salesky, Sabrina Mielke, Aditi Chaudhary, Giuseppe G. A. Celano, Edoardo M. Ponti, Ekaterina Vylomova, Ryan Cotterell, and Isabelle Augenstein. 2020. SIGTYP 2020 Shared Task: Prediction of Typological Features. In *Proceedings of the Second Workshop on Computational Research in Linguistic Typology.* Association for Computational Linguistics.

Reed Coke, Ben King, and Dragomir Radev. 2016. Classifying syntactic regularities for hundreds of languages. *arXiv preprint arXiv:1603.08016.*

Chris Collins and Richard Kayne. 2009. Syntactic structures of the world's languages. `http://sswl.railsplayground.net/..`

Hal Daumé III. 2009. Non-parametric bayesian areal linguistics. *arXiv preprint arXiv:0906.5114.*

Hal Daumé III and Lyle Campbell. 2009. A bayesian model for discovering typological implications. *arXiv preprint arXiv:0907.0785.*

Martin Haspelmath Hartmann, Iren and editors Bradley Taylor. 2013. Valency Patterns Leipzig.

Martin Haspelmath. 2009. *The typological database of the World Atlas of Language Structures.* Berlin: Walter de Gruyter.

Patrick Littell, David R Mortensen, Ke Lin, Katherine Kairis, Carlisle Turner, and Lori Levin. 2017. Uriel and lang2vec: Representing languages as typological, geographical, and phylogenetic vectors. In *Proceedings of the 15th Conference of the European Chapter of the Association for Computational Linguistics: Volume 2, Short Papers*, pages 8–14.

Ian Maddieson, Sébastien Flavier, Egidio Marsico, Christophe Coupé, and François Pellegrino. 2013. Lapsyd: lyon-albuquerque phonological systems database. In *INTERSPEECH*, pages 3022–3026.

Chaitanya Malaviya, Graham Neubig, and Patrick Littell. 2017. Learning language representations for typology prediction. *arXiv preprint arXiv:1707.09569.*

Philippe Maurer Martin Haspelmath Michaelis, Susanne Maria and editors Magnus Huber. 2013. Atlas of Pidgin and Creole Language Structures Online.

Sebastian Ruder. 2017. An overview of multitask learning in deep neural networks. corr abs/1706.05098. *arXiv preprint arXiv:1706.05098.*

Ashish Vaswani, Noam Shazeer, Niki Parmar, Jakob Uszkoreit, Llion Jones, Aidan N Gomez, Łukasz Kaiser, and Illia Polosukhin. 2017. Attention is all you need. In *Advances in neural information processing systems*, pages 5998–6008.

A Appendix 1

Table 3: Feature-wise accuracy.

Begin of Table	
WALS Feature	Accuracy
Order_of_Person_Markers_on_the_Verb	0.4307692307692308
Order_of_Subject,_Object_and_Verb	0.43855421686746987
Order_of_Adposition_and_Noun_Phrase	0.4805970149253731
Position_of_Case_Affixes	0.4445945945945946
Minor_morphological_means_of_signaling_negation	0.6905405405405406
Position_of_Tense-Aspect_Affixes	0.5986842105263158
Order_of_Degree_Word_and_Adjective	0.5923076923076923
Postnominal_relative_clauses	0.65
Postverbal_Negative_Morphemes	0.6054054054054054
Person_Marking_on_Adpositions	0.5115384615384615
Weight_Factors_in_Weight-Sensitive_Stress_Systems	0.35
Presence_of_Uncommon_Consonants	0.6487804878048781
Preverbal_Negative_Morphemes	0.5297297297297298
Negative_Morphemes	0.44
Absence_of_Common_Consonants	0.5804878048780487
Polar_Questions	0.5345454545454545
Glottalized_Consonants	0.6317073170731707
Voicing_in_Plosives_and_Fricatives	0.5634146341463415
Position_of_Negative_Word_With_Respect_to_Subject,_Object,_and_Verb	0.4846153846153846
Passive_Constructions	0.616
Front_Rounded_Vowels	0.6487804878048781
Gender_Distinctions_in_Independent_Personal_Pronouns	0.6192307692307693
Rhythm_Types	0.506896551724138
Tone	0.6631578947368421
Position_of_Polar_Question_Particles	0.45769230769230773
Order_of_Numeral_and_Noun	0.4830985915492958
Pronominal_and_Adnominal_Demonstratives	0.6125
Fixed_Stress_Locations	0.49
Finger_and_Hand	0.6348837209302325
Verbal_Person_Marking	0.45769230769230773
Third_Person_Zero_of_Verbal_Person_Marking	0.5923076923076923
Order_of_Subject_and_Verb	0.6263157894736842
Weight-Sensitive_Stress	0.3325
Order_of_Object_and_Verb	0.48404255319148937
Order_of_Relative_Clause_and_Noun	0.586046511627907
Alignment_of_Verbal_Person_Marking	0.5923076923076923
Position_of_Pronominal_Possessive_Affixes	0.4148148148148148
Voicing_and_Gaps_in_Plosive_Systems	0.5975609756097561
Consonant-Vowel_Ratio	0.5463414634146342
Expression_of_Pronominal_Subjects	0.5630434782608695
Intensifiers_and_Reflexive_Pronouns	0.525
Consonant_Inventories	0.35853658536585364
Vowel_Quality_Inventories	0.5634146341463415
Syllable_Structure	0.44545454545454544

Continuation of Table 3	
WALS Feature	Accuracy
Order_of_Genitive_and_Noun	0.5936708860759494
Order_of_Adjective_and_Noun	0.5530864197530864
Third_Person_Pronouns_and_Demonstratives	0.4421052631578947
Lateral_Consonants	0.5634146341463415
Prefixing_vs._Suffixing_in_Inflectional_Morphology	0.49482758620689654
The_Position_of_Negative_Morphemes_in_Object-Initial_Languages	0.35
Distance_Contrasts_in_Demonstratives	0.4529411764705883
Order_of_Negative_Morpheme_and_Verb	0.4824324324324324
Hand_and_Arm	0.574
Uvular_Consonants	0.4609756097560976
Position_of_Interrogative_Phrases_in_Content_Questions	0.6234375000000001
SONegV_Order	0.45862068965517244
NegSOV_Order	0.6758620689655173
The_Position_of_Negative_Morphemes_in_SOV_Languages	0.2930232558139535
The_Associative_Plural	0.49411764705882355
SNegOV_Order	0.6758620689655173
Order_of_Adverbial_Subordinator_and_Clause	0.525
The_Prohibitive	0.49677419354838714
SOVNeg_Order	0.4117647058823529
Coding_of_Nominal_Plurality	0.5101694915254237
The_Morphological_Imperative	0.6363636363636364
Order_of_Demonstrative_and_Noun	0.5272727272727273
Comitatives_and_Instrumentals	0.6481481481481481
Ditransitive_Constructions:_The_Verb_'Give'	0.5303030303030303
'Want'_Complement_Subjects	0.5727272727272728
Order_of_Object,_Oblique,_and_Verb	0.48125
Noun_Phrase_Conjunction	0.6588235294117647
Predicative_Possession	0.24705882352941178
Definite_Articles	0.41621621621621624
Languages_with_two_Dominant_Orders_of_Subject,_Object,_and_Verb	0.7
Zero_Copula_for_Predicate_Nominals	0.40384615384615385
Languages_with_different_word_order_in_negative_clauses	0.0
Tea	0.6363636363636364
Nominal_and_Locational_Predication	0.5384615384615385
Predicative_Adjectives	0.4307692307692308
Nominal_and_Verbal_Conjunction	0.45454545454545454544
Cultural_Categories_of_Languages_with_Identity_of_'Finger'_and_'Hand'	0.56
Inclusive/Exclusive_Forms_in_Pama-Nyungan	0.385
Occurrence_of_Nominal_Plurality	0.364
Indefinite_Pronouns	0.564516129032258
Indefinite_Articles	0.3612903225806452
The_Optative	0.6
Ordinal_Numerals	0.5
Semantic_Distinctions_of_Evidentiality	0.5352941176470588
Multiple_Negative_Constructions_in_SOV_Languages	0.0
Coding_of_Evidentiality	0.5558823529411765
Politeness_Distinctions_in_Pronouns	0.7
Systems_of_Gender_Assignment	0.4869565217391304

Continuation of Table 3

WALS Feature	Accuracy
Locus_of_Marking:_Whole-language_Typology	0.35
Asymmetrical_Case-Marking	0.4117647058823529
M_in_First_Person_Singular	0.56
Sex-based_and_Non-sex-based_Gender_Systems	0.6391304347826087
Number_of_Cases	0.5764705882352941
Reduplication	0.5764705882352941
Numeral_Classifiers	0.5833333333333334
Number_of_Possessive_Nouns	0.7
Applicative_Constructions	0.35
M_in_Second_Person_Singular	0.56
Locus_of_Marking_in_Possessive_Noun_Phrases	0.5055555555555555
Possessive_Classification	0.48125
Other_Roles_of_Applied_Objects	0.4
M-T_Pronouns	0.665
N-M_Pronouns	0.595
Locus_of_Marking_in_the_Clause	0.4666666666666667
Adjectives_without_Nouns	0.4666666666666667
Antipassive_Constructions	0.525
Zero_Marking_of_A_and_P_Arguments	0.7
Productivity_of_the_Antipassive_Construction	0.5133333333333333
Obligatory_Possessive_Inflection	0.7
Number_of_Genders	0.5478260869565218
Nonperiphrastic_Causative_Constructions	0.6719999999999999
Plurality_in_Independent_Personal_Pronouns	0.5333333333333333
Purpose_Clauses	0.6533333333333333
Imperative-Hortative_Systems	0.7
Vowel_Nasalization	0.49411764705882355
Prenominal_relative_clauses	0.6066666666666667
SVNegO_Order	0.7
SVONeg_Order	0.7
Number_of_Non-Derived_Basic_Colour_Categories	0.4666666666666667
Red_and_Yellow	0.7
NegSVO_Order	0.5923076923076923
Green_and_Blue	0.7
Number_of_Basic_Colour_Categories	0.4666666666666667
SNegVO_Order	0.2692307692307693
The_Position_of_Negative_Morphemes_in_SVO_Languages	0.25
Negative_Indefinite_Pronouns_and_Predicate_Negation	0.5384615384615385
Utterance_Complement_Clauses	0.7
'When'_Clauses	0.55
The_Velar_Nasal	0.49
Optional_Double_Negation_in_SOV_languages	0.0
Optional_Double_Negation	0.0
Para-Linguistic_Usages_of_Clicks	0.4666666666666667
Distributive_Numerals	0.23333333333333334
Verb-Initial_with_Preverbal_Negative	0.35
The_Position_of_Negative_Morphemes_in_Verb-Initial_Languages	0.175
Reason_Clauses	0.6416666666666666

Continuation of Table 3	
WALS Feature	Accuracy
Verb-Initial_with_Clause-Final_Negative	0.7
Alignment_of_Case_Marking_of_Pronouns	0.4666666666666667
Alignment_of_Case_Marking_of_Full_Noun_Phrases	0.525
Inclusive/Exclusive_Distinction_in_Verbal_Inflection	0.5923076923076923
Syncretism_in_Verbal_Person/Number_Marking	0.5384615384615385
Numeral_Bases	0.4307692307692308
Case_Syncretism	0.4307692307692308
Inclusive/Exclusive_Distinction_in_Independent_Pronouns	0.7
Relativization_on_Subjects	0.7
Action_Nominal_Constructions	0.4375
Periphrastic_Causative_Constructions	0.56
Situational_Possibility	0.6363636363636364
Relativization_on_Obliques	0.3
Symmetric_and_Asymmetric_Standard_Negation	0.5055555555555555
Epistemic_Possibility	0.5384615384615385
Subtypes_of_Asymmetric_Standard_Negation	0.4277777777777778
Overlap_between_Situational_and_Epistemic_Modal_Marking	0.44545454545454544
Comparative_Constructions	0.6222222222222222
The_Future_Tense	0.7
Perfective/Imperfective_Aspect	0.5090909090909091
The_Perfect	0.7
The_Past_Tense	0.44545454545454544
Suppletion_in_Imperatives_and_Hortatives	0.63
Exponence_of_Selected_Inflectional_Formatives	0.63
Genitives,_Adjectives_and_Relative_Clauses	0.5
Verbal_Number_and_Suppletion	0.56
Suppletion_According_to_Tense_and_Aspect	0.7
Reciprocal_Constructions	0.5133333333333333
Inflectional_Synthesis_of_the_Verb	0.7
Fusion_of_Selected_Inflectional_Formatives	0.38888888888888895
Conjunctions_and_Universal_Quantifiers	0.175
Exponence_of_Tense-Aspect-Mood_Inflection	0.56
Obligatory_Double_Negation_in_SOV_languages	0.23333333333333334
Obligatory_Double_Negation	0.23333333333333334
Multiple_Negative_Constructions_in_SVO_Languages	0.7
Double_negation_in_verb-initial_languages	0.0
Internally-headed_relative_clauses	0.7
Optional_Double_Negation_in_SVO_languages	0.0
End of Table	

Association for Computational Linguistics
209 N. Eighth Street
Stroudsburg, Pennsylvania 18360

ISBN 978-1-7138-2003-1
9 781713 820031

CURRAN ASSOCIATES INC.
proceedings.com